THIS BOOK WILL TEACH YOU TO

# START A NEW JOB STRONG

## THE INSIDER'S GUIDE TO GETTING UP TO SPEED FAST AT YOUR NEW JOB

13-digit ISBN: 978-1-95151-107-4
10-digit ISBN: 1-95151-107-4

This book may be ordered by mail from the publisher. Please include $5.99 for postage and handling. Please support your local bookseller first!

Books published by Whalen Book Works are available at special discounts when purchased in bulk. For more information, please email us at info@whalenbookworks.com.

Whalen Book Works
68 North Street
Kennebunkport, ME 04046

www.whalenbookworks.com

Printed in China
1 2 3 4 5 6 7 8 9 0

First Edition

"A NEW JOB IS LIKE A BLANK BOOK AND YOU ARE THE AUTHOR."

—UNKNOWN

# CONTENTS

# INTRODUCTION

This short and handy book gives you the basics to be ready for your new place of employment. A new job can be exciting, but also nerve-racking: Will you fit in? Will you be able to do everything you said you could? Will you get along with your new coworkers? Thankfully, this guide gives you tips and techniques to make the most of your work, from orientation through the first one hundred days!

*This Book Will Teach You to Start a New Job Strong* delivers timely and needed advice about one of the most important phases of your work: your first ninety days. Acing the interview and getting hired are just the beginning. Before you even start, you may have a seemingly endless assortment of paperwork to fill out, orientation, onboarding meetings, and other ways to help you get up to speed. But what about other things, like planning for your commute, fitting in with your new environment, cultivating new working relationships with your coworkers, figuring out where the bathrooms and break rooms are, and where the best places to get lunch can be found in your vicinity? Never fear, help is at hand!

Starting a new job can be both exciting and stressful, and you may feel like a fish out of water (even if you're not flapping about). This information will help you to get into the right frame of mind to go in from day one and show them what you can do.

With the tips and advice in *This Book Will Teach You to Start a New Job Strong*, you'll be able to tackle everything your new job throws at you, impress your boss, be at ease with your new coworkers, and be well on your way to settling in and feeling at home in no time! This small guide won't tell you how to succeed at a tech company, a law office, or a government job, since each reader will be coming from a different background. Rather, it will give tips and advice that can be used in any field of employment to help you get the most out of your first few weeks and months.

The book is divided into chapters arranged by subject for ease of browsing. The information gives you a starting point, basic how-tos to get you started. Consider this information to be a reference and handy guide when you want to check out something about a specific topic quickly. Feel free to browse through the book wherever you like, and read it in whatever order works for you. You may find some of the information to be more relevant than other entries, but there should be something here for everyone who is beginning a new job. Of course, a small book has some limits to what it can offer, but use it as a starting point for further study and research. Keep in mind that this book is not a substitute for legal or other advice, and if you need additional help on any of the subjects herein, you can use the Resources section at the end. This section offers more helpful reading and a list of websites with legal information, often directly from government sources. Consider this book to be your handy one-volume introduction to the confusing but also rewarding journey of starting your new job!

"Every day is a chance to begin again. Don't focus on the failures of yesterday; start today with positive thoughts and expectations."

—CATHERINE PULSIFER

# CHAPTER 1

# GETTING THE JOB AND NAVIGATING YOUR FIRST FEW DAYS!

If you've just been hired, congratulations! Your hard work (whether in college or in previous jobs) has paid off, and someone (or several someones) has noticed and wants to give you a chance. This is an opportunity to make a new start, to learn new things, and to make your mark. And just maybe start a new career that you'll love. Starting a new job is exciting, but it can be nerve-racking. You may feel overwhelmed in your first week, with so much new information to take in, people to meet, routines to learn, names to remember . . . it's a bit of a whirlwind, but with preparation, you can navigate through it just fine and come out on top by that first Friday. This chapter covers some of what you can expect in your first few days and how to approach it all so that you're feeling confident and ready to face your new challenges.

# CONGRATULATIONS, YOU'VE BEEN OFFERED A JOB! WHAT DO YOU DO NOW?

You've received the notice that the interview went great, and that the company loves you and wants you to start on a specific date! Awesome! Break out the bubbly or your celebratory drink of choice! Except . . . what if you've been offered more than one job? What if two different jobs both have advantages and disadvantages? What if there are things in the employment terms and conditions that you're not so thrilled with? Here are some questions to ask yourself before and after you accept an offer.

- **Is this job the one you really want?** You may have applied at several companies, and this is the first one that got back to you. Is it your first choice? Are you still waiting to hear from someone else? You may have a limited time to accept the offer, but if you know that one or more others may be coming, be careful about accepting any offer too soon. They will likely give you a time limit for your answer.

- **What are this job's advantages and drawbacks?** Every job comes with both good and less good aspects. The salary may be great, but it may be a dreadful commute. It might be just down the block from you, but more formal than you're comfortable with. You'll need to make a list of the pros and cons of the job and see which outweighs the other. If a less desirable offer is the only one you get, you may feel pressured to take it, no matter what. Just be aware going in that there may be some problems you'll have to deal with right away.

- **Where is the job located?** Maybe you shoot the moon and apply for a job in another city or province, or even country. But what happens if they like you and want an interview, or, even better, to hire you? Are you prepared to relocate for a job? It might be a fantastic opportunity, but you'll have to do some soul-searching first to see if it's really the right course to take. This can be a huge change and not one to make lightly.

- **Is anything negotiable?** Perhaps you've been offered a dream job, but the salary is a bit lower than you wanted, or the benefits are not quite as good, or they want you to work unusual hours. Check and see if any of this is negotiable or if it's a "take it or leave it" offer. If you are young and have little work experience, it's more likely that you'll have to take what they give you, but there may be some room for flexibility, especially if they see you as promising and someone who can grow with the company. Be careful about getting demanding, though, or you'll soon find yourself without any offer at all!

- **Are you sure?** When you are ready to sign an agreement or accept an offer, be sure that it's right for you. It's extremely unethical (and even illegal in some cases) to back out of an offer you've signed an agreement for, if a job you like better comes along a few days later. Again, sometimes you don't have a choice; you have a limited-time opportunity to take an offer, and you feel you have to do it. But just be sure it feels right for you. Check in with friends and family and get their opinions. They might be able to offer you some insights and advice you hadn't thought of.

Getting a job offer is exciting and rewarding, but take the time to consider all aspects of it before saying yes. You'll be doing yourself and the company a favor, and ensuring that it's the right fit for you and your goals.

# HAVING THE RIGHT MINDSET: SEVEN TIPS

**Going into a new job can be intimidating, but there are things you can do to make the process easier. But simply changing how you think about your experience can have real-world benefits. Here are some attitudes and practices to keep in mind as you start out.**

1. **Adopt a growth mindset approach.** Enter into this new phase of your life with the attitude that you want to learn and grow, not only professionally but also personally. It isn't just about a new (and maybe even bigger) paycheck; it's about all of the other experiences you'll have and not only what you'll gain, but what you'll be able to offer, too. Go in with the idea of becoming a better person.

2. **Think about what's next.** Getting a new job may make you feel like celebrating, and you should! But also be prepared for what's about to come. You know that you'll be entering into unfamiliar territory, so get yourself in the frame of mind to deal with that. Look out for chances to be proactive, not just reactive. Do the work you are assigned, of course, but also see if there are other areas where you can make suggestions and contributions, even right from day one.

3. **Go in ready to learn.** Have an open mind and be ready to absorb everything that's thrown at you (and it will probably be a lot!). In fact, you'll likely have too much to take in all at once. That's OK. Be patient with yourself, but always strive to learn a bit more every day.

4. **Ask questions, and then ask more.**  People who are already there will know much more about the workplace and its processes than you do. Ask your new coworkers about anything you're unsure of. Ask your boss. Reach out to any and all people, and take their advice and information with gratitude. Be sure to find out what your boss expects from you today, this week, this month. Ask what you can do to meet and exceed those expectations. Let your boss know that you're ready from day one.

5. **Take stock of your skills and what you want to get from the experience.** You were obviously hired because of a combination of skills and other qualities, so review what you bring to the table. You'll undoubtedly pick up many new skills along the way, so think about of how those will be useful in your career going forward. You may be receiving some on-the-job training for certain tasks that will be valuable in the future. Maybe the skills you already have can be sharpened and expanded. Look for opportunities to improve. Are certain specializations going to be more in demand in the future? Can you take advantage of that?

6. **Keep track of your progress at the beginning.** How did your first day go? Your first week? Your first month? What went right, and what could be improved? Ask your boss how you're progressing in the first couple of weeks. What are you doing well? What would they like to see more of?

7. **Plan ahead for thirty, sixty, and ninety days.** Based on the work you're doing and what's expected of you, set realistic goals for your job and your own career. Periodic check-ins are a great way to monitor your own progress, independently of any outside review. Set realistic goals for yourself and meet them, or even exceed them, if you can (see "Setting Realistic Work Goals from the Start," page 61).

# GETTING UP TO SPEED

When you step into a new workplace, there will almost certainly be a lot to learn. From simple things like the location of the bathrooms and break room, to more complex issues of how tasks are performed and how the workplace functions, you'll probably feel bombarded with new information. Here are some tips for getting up to speed quickly without feeling like you've been overloaded.

- **Make lists of what you need to learn.** Write down everything and prioritize it, with whatever is most important first. Do this, even if your new job is similar to one you've had before or if you know the subject (such as computer programming) very well. There will be different ways of doing things, proprietary information, and any number of other factors to consider. You may have a lot to learn about the company itself, depending on your position, so again, make sure that the most important information is your priority.

- **Understand your own learning process.** Do you learn new information quickly? Do you need to take more time to absorb it all? Are you more visual? Auditory? Ask yourself these questions and be honest. How well you process all the new material that will be coming your way will affect how well you can get to work on it.

- **Read any literature you're given, more than once.** You may receive an employee handbook or some similar guide. It will probably explain a number of things about company policies, locations of important items, and so on. Make sure you know it well, and keep it with you. If your new job doesn't offer something like this, ask your boss if there is any helpful literature or handouts that you might need.

- **Take in the office environment.** Try to learn about the workplace culture so you can fit in better. Is it formal? Causal? How do your new coworkers interact? There may be a rigid hierarchy, or things may be more loosely structured. It will all depend on the kind of company it is, of course, but the more you can observe it like a nature documentary, the better a sense you'll have of your own role and required behavior going forward.

- **Keep track of what's expected of you and when.** In these early days, make more lists or use a software calendar (or similar program) to set your tasks and deadlines. Eventually, you'll probably get a feel for the workflow and won't need outside help, but at the beginning, being able to see what's due when will save you a lot of hassle and stress.

- **Be ready to contribute.** You were hired because you're valuable, and your employer wants you to be a part of the team going forward. It's fine to hold back and listen and absorb, but don't be so reticent that you never feel you can contribute. People *want* to hear what you have to say, so dig in and go for it! The more you feel comfortable contributing to projects, the more you'll feel like you're a valid part of the group, and everyone else will, too.

- **Be aware of your own needs and shortcomings.** Maybe you have trouble asking for advice. Maybe you have a hard time introducing yourself to new people. Time management might be a problem (if so, see pages 25–26). That's fine; everyone is different, and no one is perfect. But being aware of any potential drawbacks that you might bring to the job will help you in dealing with them and not letting them hold you back.

- **Don't neglect yourself.** The new job is your main focus, but don't let it be the only thing in your life. Being able to maintain a sense of balance and continuing to do what you've always done in your personal life will give you a greater sense of continuity and the feeling that you can tackle whatever tasks the job throws at you.

> **"Your talent determines what you can do. Your motivation determines how much you are willing to do. Your attitude determines how well you do it."**
>
> *—LOU HOLTZ*

# PAPERS, FORMS, AND MORE PAPERS

Starting a new job usually involves more than just filling out an application and handing in a resume. Depending on the type of business you're working for, you may have any number of legal and financial papers to read through and sign. It's a boring part of the process, but a necessary one. So here is a short list of the documents you'll need and the ones you're most likely to find as you wade through the pile of things you're expected to read. You'll usually receive any necessary documents in the first day or two of your employment.

- **Social Insurance Number (SIN).** Many Canadians have these almost from birth, a nine-digit number that makes you eligible to work in Canada and to obtain government benefits. You *must* have an SIN to work legally in Canada.

- **If you're a Canadian resident but not a citizen, you will need to provide an original copy of one of the following to prove your eligibility to work.** Doing so will allow you to apply for an SIN:

  - A Permanent Resident Card

  - A Confirmation of Permanent Residence

  - A Record of Landing

- **A Verification of Landing**

- **A Verification of Status**

- **When you have your SIN.** Assuming that this is all taken care of and you have an SIN, your new employer will be required to record that number within three days of you starting your job. This is something you can assume will be taken care of on your behalf and is your employer's responsibility. If you have any concerns, ask and make sure that it's been done.

- **Tax forms.** You will need to fill out the TD1 form (Personal Tax Credit Return), both the federal form and one for the province where you reside and will be working. These forms are used to determine how much tax will be deducted from your pay. If you are working in Quebec, you'll need to fill out the TD1 for the federal and Form TP1015.3-V (Source Deductions Return) for the province. If you have any questions, ask your employer or refer to the government tax site (see the Resources section).

- **A job offer document.** Not every employer has one of these, but you may be asked to sign an acceptance agreement for your new job, not unlike a contract, which details things like hours, salary, benefits, job duties, etc. These agreements are very useful so that there are no misunderstandings later on. If you do receive one of these documents, read it thoroughly and make sure you understand it (you'll probably be given a copy). It may also confirm that your job complies with labor standards, both at the federal and provincial level.

- **Proprietary agreements.** If you are working on software or scientific research, or any number of projects where the work involves patents or is otherwise secretive, you may be ask to sign a nondisclosure agreement. These are often requested if the company is working on something proprietary, such as new pharmaceuticals or revolutionary software. The point is that they don't want employees discussing their work with potential competitors. You'll be required to sign and expected to take it seriously. If you break the agreement, even by accident, you may face legal troubles, fines, and even prosecution. These kinds of agreements usually extend past your period of employment. If you leave the job after two years, for example, you are not allowed to discuss what it was you were working on, perhaps forever.

[
**"It isn't necessary to imagine the world ending in fire or ice—there are two other possibilities: one is paperwork, and the other is nostalgia."**
]
**—FRANK ZAPPA**

# WHAT TO EXPECT AT ORIENTATION

**If you're starting a new job at a larger company, you may be asked to attend an orientation session to help you ease in to the job. This might be a few hours, or take up a whole day or even the whole week, and can be very useful in getting yourself quite literally oriented to your new environment. It might happen before you start work, or it might be what you do on your first day. You may well be one of several new hires, or there may only be a few of you. Here are some useful tips for making the most of it.**

- **Check in ahead of time.** It's a good idea to check in with your new employer to see if there is anything that you need to prepare for. More than likely, they will have told you everything you need to know, but it doesn't hurt to ask. If the company gave you an employee handbook, read through it before the orientation. Even if they go through it while you're there, it's good to have a sense of what's expected going in.

- **Arrive on time, or better yet, be early.** Punctuality counts, and you want to make a good first impression, so it's important to be prepared and ready. Being early won't hurt you, but being late is never a good look.

- **Dress for success.** Make sure that you are adhering to the company's dress code, even if this is technically not your first day on the job. If you don't yet know what the code is, ask. Again, you want to make a good first impression. Even of the company leans more toward business casual, it's not a bad idea to dress up a little bit more at first.

- **Be ready to take lots of notes.** Whether you use pen and paper or your laptop, there will likely be a lot of information new to you, so be ready. It's also good for writing down any questions you have during sessions, so that you don't forget to ask them later.

- **Make sure you are ready to fill out any necessary forms.** You may be asked to provide your tax information at orientation, so bring any relevant information with you (such as your SIN, if you don't know it).

- **Be prepared to ask a lot of questions.** There will certainly be things that are left out, no matter how thorough the orientation is. Don't hesitate to ask about anything you need to know or are confused about.

- **Find out what the food situation is.** There will likely be a lunch break, but check to see if food is provided; sometimes it is, sometimes not. If not, you'll have to bring your own or find a nearby place to get lunch. The last thing you want is to be hungry, grumpy, and irritated for the afternoon session!

- **Give each session your full attention.** There may be more than one presenter or speaker at your orientation. You may hear from the department head, the human resources person, your boss, or perhaps even a vice president or the CEO. Be sure to be attentive to any and all presenters, since each of them will be there for a specific reason.

- **Ask what else is expected of you.** At the end of the orientation, inquire about what the next step is. Are you finished with introductions? When do you start work? If you have any lingering questions, now is the time to ask them.

> **"I always did something I was a little not ready to do. I think that's how you grow. When there's that moment of 'Wow, I'm not really sure I can do this,' and you push through those moments, that's when you have a breakthrough."**
>
> **—MARISSA MAYER**

# YOUR NEW ROUTINE: MORNINGS AND COMMUTE

Starting a new, on-site job will mean a shift in your routine, perhaps a dramatic one. If you're fresh out of university and used to sleeping in until 11:00 a.m., this might come as a real shock! You'll have to make some pretty big changes to accommodate your new place of employment, and if you're not a morning person, this can seem more than a little daunting. So here are some suggestions on how to make the transition a bit easier, none of which involve you still being able to sleep in until 11:00 a.m., sorry to say!

- **Practice getting up early.** This may sound a bit silly, but if you're not used to early rising, it will definitely come as a shock when your new job begins! If you have a week or so before the big day, try waking up at the time you'd normally be getting up to go to work. It will make the transition much easier. If you have enough time to prepare, try getting up a little bit earlier each morning until the big day, so that you can ease into it a bit more smoothly.

- **Once you're settled in, keep getting up at that time.** Yes, even on weekends, at least for a while. You want your body to get used to rising at that hour, and if you slip right back into sleeping until noon on Saturdays and Sundays, it's going to take a lot longer to get used to your new schedule. Also, Mondays will seem pretty brutal if you do that!

- **Find out exactly what your commute requires.** If you are driving, does your workplace have parking? If not, is parking available and is it free, or do you have to pay for it? If you're taking a bus or train/subway, how far away is the stop from your office? How far away is the stop from where you live? Will you have to transfer from one bus to another? Don't leave these kinds of uncertainties until the last minute.

- **Practice your new commute.** It doesn't matter if you're driving, taking a bus, or using other public transportation, take a few days to practice the commute beforehand, at the same time that you expect to go in. It will give you a good sense of how much time it will take to get to your office, what delays might happen, and anything else that may come up. This will also be helpful if there are specific bus numbers or routes that you need to take and are unsure about. Don't leave that uncertainty until your first day!

- **A short nap can help in the beginning.** No, probably not at your desk, but if you're exhausted when you get home, a short nap can revive you. But be careful not to make it more than ten to twenty minutes, or you'll wake up feeling groggy and like you're jet-lagged. The point is to give yourself a little boost, not to reset your biological clock to another time zone!

- **Exercise can help, too.** If you work out or do other things to keep fit, keep doing them, not only for your health but also to help regulate your sleep schedule. If you don't exercise, consider taking up something that you can do at least a few days a week. If you're sitting at a desk all day, being able to get up and move will provide real physical benefits as well.

# BEING ON TIME, EVERY TIME

Some people are naturally great at being on time; they show up early, are fully prepared, never leave anyone waiting, and are general all-around time heroes. Then there are the rest of us. We all know that being punctual is desirable, and we all know we should try to be, but so often, we fail. And yet we always appreciate when people make the effort to be on time for us; just think of how annoyed you can get if you end up having to wait for someone, especially if it's something you have to do over and over.
And if you are late to work a few too many times, your employer won't just be annoyed; they'll fire you. So if you struggle with time, here is some advice to mastering it.

- **Get to know how long your commute takes.**

As mentioned in the previous entry, practice your new commute. This will give you an idea of the total time involved in getting from point A to point B. Expect that some days this will take longer. A bus may be delayed, you may get stuck in traffic, weather could interfere, or there could be a problem on the rail lines. One rule of thumb is to figure out the time your trip takes and then add an extra 25 percent to it. Allow for that extra amount every day. Most days you'll probably get to work a bit early, but just in case something does go wrong, you'll be prepared. If a truly bad traffic jam or other unforeseen incident happens that's beyond your control, be sure to call into your office and let them know. Things happen, and no one is likely to be upset when the occasional delay happens. Just be sure that this is the real reason and you're not using it as an excuse to be late!

- **Be up early enough that you don't have to rush around.** Again, this should be obvious, but leaving the alarm until the last possible minute and then having to dash around your home before sailing out the door isn't going to do you or your workplace any good. Consider trying an alarm that wakes you up a bit more gently, so that you're not shocked into wakefulness. Also, forget about the snooze button—the snooze button is your enemy; resist the snooze button at all costs. Lay out your clothes the night before, have your lunch made (if you're taking it), and have all of your work materials packed and ready to go. Do everything you need to do to make your mornings as easy as possible.

- **Don't forget to sleep!** Just because you have to get up early doesn't mean that you should be failing to get enough sleep. You'll just have to adjust your bedtime to make sure that you do get enough. In terms of hours of sleep, you probably know what your own needs are to not feel zonked. But you want to feel better than just functioning. Seriously, don't neglect sleeping just because you're young and you think you can take it, or you find that you're being pressured to sleep less and work more. There's nothing noble or cool about sleep loss, and it can have long-term effects on your health, sooner than you might think.

- **Always remember that you're being paid to be at your workplace at a given time.** If other motivations don't work for you, just keep in mind that your company is paying your salary, and in exchange they expect you to be at work at the designated time, ready to work. You may find that over time, there will be some flexibility in scheduling (you may be able to come in later and work later, or even work from home now and then), but in the beginning, you want to impress, so make every effort to be punctual, or even better, to be early.

# EIGHT STEPS TO SURVIVING YOUR FIRST DAY

You've been hired, you've made it through orientation, you've signed all the forms, and now you're ready to start. Day one is here—help! Settling into your first actual day may be exciting and anxiety-provoking. But if you've paid attention to the advice given so far, you'll be ready. Here are some more tips to make the most of your first day on the job.

1. **Be on time.** As we've covered before, this is essential. Being a few minutes early is fine, but don't show up, say, a half hour early. That might look a bit weird, unless you've been requested to show up early on day one for necessary paperwork.

2. **Remember to take any relevant paperwork.** Is there anything you need to bring? From IDs to orientation material, make sure that all of your documents are ready the night before.

3. **Remember to take any relevant personal items.** Take stock of other essentials: a water bottle, medications, snacks, a little extra cash, anything else that you might need or want. You'll get a better sense of your daily needs after a few days, but be prepared at first.

4. **Go in with a positive attitude.** Obviously, this makes sense. Smile, be friendly, be ready for introductions, and keep an open mind. Showing others that you're ready to join them and work with them is a great way of bonding right away, and will help you fit in early.

**5. Greet everyone pleasantly and sincerely.**
Smile, shake hands, and be willing to meet any and all
people. These are now your coworkers, and it's essential
that you get off to a good start with them. It will take some
time to remember names and who does what, but make the effort to
do your introductions correctly, and you'll be remembered well.

**6. Be ready to explain who you are and what you do
briefly.** Have a short intro ready so that when people ask you about
yourself, you can tell them without rambling or going on too long. Keep
it to twenty or thirty seconds, and practice it ahead of time. You want it
in your head so that you can say it with ease and not sound like you're
giving anyone a memorized speech.

**7. Just take it all in.** Whether you are starting right into work or doing
orientation, be open and ready to absorb new information.

**8. Practice self-care.** You'll probably have a lot thrown at you on day
one, so be ready to take care of yourself when you get home, too. A good
meal, a long shower, a nice bath—all could be a good way to unwind after
the whirlwind of the first day.

# INTRODUCTIONS MADE EASY: HOW TO SAY HELLO AND REMEMBER WHO EVERYONE IS

In your first few days, you'll probably be meeting a lot of new people. Depending on how big your company is, you may have individuals from many different departments that you'll be interacting and working with. You'll probably be introduced to some of them, and with others you may want to take the initiative and reach out to them on your own. Here is a handy guide to making introductions smooth and easy.

- **In your first few days, your boss will probably take you around and introduce you to everyone you'll be working with.** If this doesn't happen, it should. Or maybe someone will be designated to take you around and do the introductions.

- **When being introduced, make eye contact, shake their hand, and repeat their name back to them:** "Mark, I'm Susan, nice to meet you!" This simple act is friendly and lets you start making a bond right from the start. Seriously, don't underestimate it. Repeating their name back to them is also a good way to help you remember who they are (see below).

- **Send a follow-up email to your new coworkers and any important people that you meet.** This is a great way to cement the bond you've started making and further helps you remember who's who.

- **Take the initiative and introduce yourself, if you feel confident to do it.** It's fine to take the initiative and do some introductions on your own. Let them know who you are and what you'll be doing.

- **Other employees may stop by to introduce themselves.** You may find over your first few days that various people will take the time to introduce themselves to you, especially if they are in other departments but might be working with you eventually. This is great and saves you the trouble! But don't hesitate to reach out to people in other departments if you know you'll be working with them at some point.

- **Some companies keep a list of employees.** If your company has one of these lists (sometimes known as an organization chart), ask for a copy. It will identify who does what and will be a big help for you at the start.

- **Tips for remembering people's names:** In the course of your introductions, you'll probably have too many names to remember all at once. You'll forget, and this is fine. Some people are great with faces but forget names easily; some are the opposite. Here are some tips for helping you retain names a bit better.

- **Again, always say their name back to them when being introduced.** Hearing it and making that connection to a given face can be very helpful in remembering their name later on. Make a point of focusing on them in that moment and giving them your full attention. It will help you retain information better.

- **Focus on something specific about that person.** Do they wear glasses? Do they have a distinct hair color or style? Anything that differentiates them can be a helpful hook for you to hang on to when filing away their name.

- **Use their name again, if you're having a chat that's longer than a brief introduction.** Asking a question is a great way to work their name into the conversation again: "So, James, you're up in IT, right? What's the best way for me to contact someone there if I have a problem?"

- **Word association sometimes helps.** If you can make a mental picture of their name with something else that reminds you of it, this is a great way to commit a name to memory. This is a classic memory technique used in language learning and other activities. Rhyming can be a good way to make an association. "Ben" sounds like "den," while "Mary" rhymes with "berry." You can be inventive and have fun with these.

- **Linking someone's name to another person can help.** Does someone have the same name as your brother or sister? That's an easy way to help you remember it. Maybe their name is the same as your favorite actor or musician.

- **What to do if you meet someone from a different cultural background.** Names come in a dazzling and splendid variety all over the world. It's highly likely, even desirable, that you will meet many people from backgrounds different than yours. Unfamiliar names can be more difficult to remember no matter what culture you come from. It's OK to ask the person to repeat it or spell it. The new person you are meeting is probably used to people not remembering their name or knowing how it's spelled, and likely won't object if you ask. It shows that you're taking the time to honor them and respect them. **Side note:** *never* comment that someone's name is "unusual" or (even worse) "exotic."

- **At the end of the conversation, say their name again:** "OK, Aarav, it was nice to meet you!"

- **Others will forget your name, too.** Forgetfulness is a two-way street, so don't expect everyone to remember who you are just because you're new. You're not likely to take offense at this, so don't worry too much about anyone else being offended because you didn't remember their name on the first try. Use the forgetfulness as a way to laugh and start a conversation.

- **If you forget a name, just ask.** Simply saying, "Sorry, I've forgotten your name; I've had so many new ones to learn this week!" should be just fine.

- **Try to remember what people prefer to be called.** Someone may be named Theodore, but prefers to be called Ted. On the other hand, if you don't know what they prefer, don't presume. Wait until you hear how others address them.

- **Make sure that you spell names correctly in emails or chat.** It's one thing that tends to make us more irritated that it probably should, but it happens. If you see that someone has misspelled your name, you're likely to get annoyed, so think about how they will feel if you do it to them. It sends the message that you couldn't be bothered to learn it, and that feels disrespectful. This is especially true when you are addressing someone higher up in the company!

# SETTLING IN AND LEARNING THE LAY OF THE LAND

As you get settled in your new position, you'll have a lot to learn, from the details of your job to how the office is laid out to things like office politics, which you're best off avoiding initially. If your environment seems a bit confusing, chances are that it'll get easier as you go, but here are some tips for settling in more easily and feeling like you fit in sooner.

- **Listen rather than acting at first.** You may have all sorts of ideas about how to help, and that's great; it's part of why you were hired! But at first it's better to take a step back and see how things are done. Ask about anything you're not sure of. There may be specific procedures or ways to present ideas and solutions, or these may have to go through certain people or departments. Get an idea of how the process works first, and then you can dazzle them with your amazing ideas!

- **Observe everything around you.** You can also pick up a lot of information just by watching. See how others interact with each other: in meetings, in the break room, at lunch, or anywhere. Again, treat it like a wildlife documentary. What do most people do at lunch? Do they go out or eat at their desks and work through? You'll get clues about office culture and politics that no one may tell you outright. If it seems prudent, you can ask, but be careful about inquiring about rivalries or bad relationships. If someone offers that kind of information to you, take it in and file it away, but don't comment initially.

- **Find ways to join conversations.** If your coworkers are chatting in the break room or the hall and it's something that you know about or like, it's perfectly fine to find a way to join in. Don't just barge into a private conversation, of course, but if it seems right, it's OK to add something. This is a way of finding common interest and creating new bonds. This is even truer if you have coworkers who need some help or information and you can provide it.

- **Find someone who is influential.** There will be some people who "move and shake" more than others in your workplace. It's a great idea to reach out to one of them and get their take on things, ask for advice and help, and offer your own. This person may be able to tell you who other key people are in the organization, and you'll be on your way to becoming a part of a network. Making key allies early on can be great for when you are working on projects later.

- **Keep an eye on arrival and leaving times.** Obviously, the normal day is 9–5 or 9–5:30, but try to get a sense of the coming and going times. If 5:00 p.m. is technically the end of the day, but everyone tends to hang around until 5:15 or 5:20, it might be good for you to do the same, at least at first. You don't want to be seen as the only one dashing out the door at 4:59 and 37 seconds. On the other hand, don't wait around just because a few others do, unless you're all in the middle of a project. You don't need to appear overeager in your first few weeks, and staying late might bring up issues of overtime.

- **Ask your boss about expectations or anything you're not sure of.** You may have already talked about this, but it's good to check in. It's a great idea to ask your boss what is expected of you in your first month, your first six months, etc. Also, if you have questions about office procedure and functions, reach out and ask. Not everything may be explained in your handbook, and your new coworkers may not know if you need help with something.

# ASSORTED QUESTIONS TO ASK YOUR NEW BOSS

Your first week will be pretty hectic, and you'll probably have a lot of information thrown at you. This is a good thing! As you're making your notes and trying to keep everything straight, there are a good number of questions you should also ask, if the answers aren't given to you in materials or by someone at HR or at your orientation. Here is a list of things you should keep in mind and ask about if you don't know.

- **Are there any unusual procedures?** Every company does things a bit differently, and it could be that some of the operating procedures for this job are different than what you're used to. Maybe there are protocols for group meetings and chats; maybe you have to log into some specific places to work on certain tasks. Maybe the person who picks up the morning coffee is the one who draws the short straw the day before! In all the hustle and bustle of getting you up to speed, there could be some basic ways of working that get overlooked and aren't explained in the training manual. Every office develops its own rituals and ways of working over a period of time. Be sure to check in and ask about anything particular to the job that seems unfamiliar or strange to you.

- **How much will you be expected to work on your own?** Some workplaces stress a lot of personal autonomy, so after you're up to speed, it's good to know what you'll be expected to do without supervision. Those are the tasks you need to really get in your head, so that you can do them without assistance. Some managers are more hands-on, but increasingly employees are expected to work on their own or in groups. Bosses have their own work to do and can't be looking after everyone else all the time.

- **What are the most important things you need to know at the start?** You've obviously been brought in for a reason. If that's to perform specific tasks or work on certain projects, ask about the most important information right up-front. Again, you may be told this, but it's always good to inquire further. You can also ask your team and coworkers, as they may have specific requests that the boss isn't aware of. Or your boss may just tell you to ask them to begin with. But in any case, make sure you know.

- **How will you be evaluated?** Every company has a different policy on this. You may have monthly or quarterly performance reviews, and it's good to know when they are coming up so you can be prepared. It's also good to know what they will be evaluating and what's expected of you, so you're not working on the wrong things. You may be evaluated on anything from job skills, to soft skills, to attendance, to overall attitude and willingness to work as a team. Try to get some information ahead of time.

- **Who was in the position before you?** This may seem a bit nosy, but it's actually useful information. If you learn that the person was promoted, you'll know that there's room for advancement at the company. If they left, you may never learn why, but it will give you some things to think about; over time, maybe you can sound out some coworkers about what went down. If the person *was* promoted, that means they're still at the company, and it would be well worth your time to reach out them. Asking for help or mentorship from the former person in your position will give you a huge advantage and head start on really getting up to speed. Your boss might even encourage you to get in touch or ask that person to reach out to you.

- **What are the opportunities for advancement?** Related to the previous point, it's OK to ask about this. If you like the company and think you may want to stick around for a while, this can give you some clarity on whether or not the job will be worth your time in the long run. You can ask also about things like education and business trips. Does the company sponsor and pay for these, at least partially? Is the company invested in getting its employees more training (on-site or elsewhere) to help them advance? If you want to go back to college at some point for an additional degree, such as an MBA, would the company be willing to work with you on that? Questions like this will give you a good idea of where you stand right from the start.

- **How do you share your ideas?** Do you take an idea to the boss directly? To a supervisor? To your team leader? If you see a way that something could work better, what's the procedure for getting it out there? Is there a more democratic approach, or should it all filter through one person? Whom do you bounce ideas off of? This is all a part of the workplace culture, and while you'll get a better sense of it as you go along, understanding the basics from day one will be very helpful.

- **How often are meetings?** Sometimes they're weekly; often they happen a lot more. You may not be required to attend every one. But be clear about when you're needed. Missing an important meeting in your first week would not be a good look! If in doubt, attend everything until you hear otherwise.

- **When is the best time of day to talk to you?** Your boss will have his or her own schedule, and may have preferred times to be contacted. Learn and respect these times, unless it's an emergency. Also, find out how they want to be reached.

- **Who are the important people to know?** This can be in your department or beyond, but try to get a sense of the key people who will be of help to you, especially in your first weeks and months. You'll likely get a list of contacts at orientation (HR, legal, etc.), but your boss may want you to connect with others that will be useful to know. The more important people you can reach out to, the better!

- **What is confidential?** This will probably be explained to you, but if any of your work is sensitive and/or protected, you won't be able to talk about it outside of the workplace. Just to be absolutely sure about this and prevent any confusion, ask about what is proprietary, if anything. Even if you don' have to sign any legal agreements, you may not be able to discuss certain aspects of work on your personal social media accounts (and to be honest, you probably shouldn't anyway). If you slip up on this, it could mean getting fired, so be clear about it!

- **As the new person, what are you most likely to get wrong?** This is a perfectly valid question to ask. If you are joining a process that is already up and running, complex, and has a learning curve, it's going to take some time for you to get used to it. Understanding where you're most likely to slip up will be a big help. Also, it shows your commitment to doing a good job at the beginning. Everyone makes mistakes, but be committed to making as few as possible.

- **How do you communicate a mistake and make efforts to correct it?** You *will* make errors, so ask your boss what the best way is to report these and how they want you to go about correcting them. Maybe you're expected to propose a solution before you even report it; maybe you need to tell your team leader first. Find out what the procedure is, so that if the worst happens, you'll be better prepared.

- **What kind of social events does the company host?** It may host several a year or none. There is usually some kind of holiday party, and maybe a summer gathering. Often, attendance at these is mandatory, especially if they are more formal (such as an annual dinner at a fancy hotel). Missing one without a valid excuse would be a big faux pas. Even if they are less structured, it's in your best interest to attend the first few, to see and be seen. These events can offer additional opportunities for networking and getting to know others at your company that you don't otherwise run into. You can ask the same question about more casual get-togethers, such as happy hours or coffee meetups. Generally, these are optional, but you should make the effort to go along while you're still new to the job.

- **What other advice does your boss have?** Ask your boss if there is anything else that can be helpful as you work your way into the company culture and take on your new role. There are always things you won't have thought of and situations that come up that you didn't anticipate. And be prepared to go back and keep asking throughout your first few weeks!

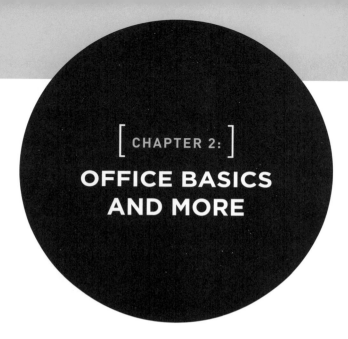

[ CHAPTER 2: ]

# OFFICE BASICS AND MORE

Every office is different, and when you step into yours, you'll have to learn the layout, the way things are done, and much more. But there are some things that are pretty consistent, mostly with how you present yourself and what you bring to the job. This chapter looks at some key points that you'll want to keep in mind in your first week and beyond.

# UNDERSTANDING YOUR NEW ROLE

Obviously, you've been hired because you have a specific set of skills that the company needs. They also decided that you have the right personality and will fit in with their company culture and future goals. You know what you'll be doing for them, basically, but what will you *really* be doing? Here are some things to keep in mind as you define your new role.

- **Learn about the company culture.** Every workplace is unique and will have its own feel. Take the time to observe yours and get a sense of how everything fits together. Since you're going to be fitting into it in your own way, you need to understand it first. What's the overall mood of the place? How formal or informal is it? How do things generally proceed from day to day? Watching for the mood and temperament during your first week will give you some extra help in defining your own role.

- **Learn about the company hierarchy.** Beyond your boss, there will be some coworkers who are more senior than others: team leaders, project managers, and so on. It's important to know where you fit in and whom you'll be reporting to. This will probably be explained to you on day one, but it's worth double-checking. You may, for example, be expected to run things by a team leader rather than your boss, so find out what the protocol is.

- **Learn company specifics.** There are almost certainly accepted ways of doing tasks, and these may be very similar or very different to what you're used to. The learning curve may feel a bit steep at first, but if you have to integrate into an existing system, you have no choice but to dive in and get up to speed. Fortunately, you'll almost certainly have lots of help with this, but you might have to stay late for a few days or take some work home with you to really get the hang of things. As always, if in doubt, ask!

- **Find out about the company's bring your own computer/device (BYOC/D) policy.** Some companies are fine with you bringing your own laptop to work on; in fact, they may even require it. Others may have laptops or even desktops that you're expected to use. This may also extend to tablets and phones. If you'd prefer to keep your work devices and your personal devices separate, ask if there are alternatives. Many companies are willing to accommodate this wish up to a point. They may even provide funds to purchase a new laptop for work only (this may be one of the benefits you get as a job perk). Whether you can use your own or are assigned company devices will be a very important piece of knowledge to know right at the start. If they don't tell you about this during the interview or a later orientation, by all means ask!

- **Check in with your boss regularly.** It's a great idea to schedule a meeting with your new boss at the end of the week to discuss your experiences, see if you are doing what's expected of you, and report how the week went for you. It's also a great chance to clarify anything you need to understand better. Ask how you're doing, what you can do better, and what will be expected of you going forward. Try to have a weekly meeting with your boss until you feel that you really have the hang of things. Your boss will appreciate you making the extra effort, and you'll feel better knowing that you're getting quality feedback.

# UNDERSTANDING COMPANY POLICIES

> **Every company will have its own set of guidelines and procedures. Some of these are firmly rooted in federal and provincial law (such as equal opportunity and discrimination policies, set hours of weekly work, and so on), while others might be particular to a given business (dress codes, lunchtimes, etc.). It's imperative that you learn these policies, especially if any of them will have an impact on you.**

- **Consult your employee handbook.** Company-specific regulations will probably all be listed in there. If your company doesn't have a handbook, ask your boss or the relevant department where you can find the needed information. If you have a handbook, it will probably contain versions of the following information:

  - **Onboarding information:** legal information, key staff members, terms of employment, safety information, etc.

  - **Code of conduct:** how you are expected to act, dress, and behave during working hours.

  - **Day-to-day information:** work hours, lunch breaks, other breaks, and so on.

  - **Information about your compensation:** how and when you are paid, deductions, bonuses, promotions, and more.

  - **Benefits specific to the job:** whatever perks they've promised and when they kick in.

- **Leave policies:** time off for emergencies, sickness, and other unforeseen events.

- **Information about leaving:** how to resign, what happens next, how your last paycheck is delivered, the ways that you can be fired, etc.

Many companies have their own detailed code-of-conduct policy that will be particular to them but that still follows various laws. This code may include specific guidelines about substance abuse, being late too frequently, disciplinary action, and more. It's in your best interest to familiarize yourself with these regulations as soon as possible.

- **Confirm that the company adheres to all legal obligations.** Do you have any special needs that need to be accommodated? Your company is legally obligated to meet certain criteria (wheelchair access, for example). Make sure that they do. To be fair, most companies have no problems doing this and are happy to comply. But it's best to find out early, so that there won't be any problems later on.

- **Learn the dress code.** Companies will vary widely on this. Some will be very casual, while others may be far more formal and traditional. Ask about this during your interview, and ask again after you're hired if you're not sure. Showing up underdressed on your first day is not only a faux pas; it could be a disaster requiring you to go home and change. Not the first impression you want to make! When in doubt, it's always better to overdress than underdress. You can always tone it down on day two. If you have a chance to tour the office before your job starts, you'll be able to get a better sense of what's appropriate to wear. This also goes for tattoos and piercings; some places may be OK with your nose ring, for example, but some businesses may ask that you take it off during work hours or wear long-sleeved shirts to cover arm tattoos. Certain things, such as cultural hairstyles or religious garb, are usually protected under antidiscrimination laws, so if you are being asked to not wear something or to radically change your appearance, check to see whether this is allowed.

- **Find out if flextime is a thing where you work—and what that means for you.** Some companies like to advertise to their prospective hires that they will have flexible hours and can set their own schedule. That sounds great in principle, but you'll need to clarify what that actually means in practice. Do people really come in later and leave later, or the opposite? Is it OK to take off two hours in the middle of the day for errands? You'll have to observe office behavior for a few days and see what the deal really is. Sorry to say, sometimes this promise is not all it's cracked up to be.

- **Is there an open-door policy?** Some companies like to proclaim that anyone at any time is welcome to make suggestions to the boss, the VP, the CEO, etc. But is this really true, or do you have to present ideas through a hierarchy? The best way to find out about this is to see if anyone actually takes advantage of it. Was a coworker able to go to the CEO or founder with a suggestion and be listened to, or did they have to run it by your immediate supervisor first? To be fair, if you're at a large company, most CEOs won't have time to listen to every idea or proposal from every employee who thinks that they're a genius. So if someone tells you this during your interview, take it with a healthy degree of skepticism.

- **Find out what the policies are on chat, email, and other office communications.** Of course, work chat and email are meant for work topics only, but even there, it's possible that there are some unwritten policies about usage. Are you expected to respond to every group message or email, for example? Is there a time limit for when you do need to respond? Ask about these things right away, so you can be in the loop and not miss any important information or assignments. If everyone else is talking about something you were supposed to have looked at two days ago, it's going to be embarrassing!

# SETTLING IN WITH YOUR NEW COWORKERS: TEN TIPS

As you settle in, you'll be meeting and working with any number of new people, from a handful in a small business to a much larger group in a bigger company. You'll gravitate to some of them more than others, but it's essential to be able to work cordially with everyone. Here are some ideas to help you after day-one introductions.

1. **Show up ready to work.** As simple as it seems, being on time and ready to go with whatever projects you're involved in is a great way to communicate that you're a part of the team and ready to contribute. Give your coworkers the same respect that you'd appreciate.

2. **Offer your ideas, but be open to new ones.**
You were brought in to contribute and you'll be expected to, but also be willing to change or modify your own suggestions and solutions. Hear everyone out, and see how you can collaborate and compromise.

3. **Bring food.** Surprise everyone with a box of donuts or snacks once in a while. Bring in coffees for your three closest associates (once you learn what they like, of course!). The occasional little treat goes a long way toward showing that you're on the team and care about others.

**4. Accept invites.** Are you asked out for lunch or coffee? Go! Especially in your first few weeks, this is a great way to get to know people and maybe meet others outside of your usual work space.

**5. Extend invites.** Be proactive and reach out to people to invite them for lunch and coffee/drinks. Show that you're invested in them, in the office and outside of it. Both accepting and extending invites will give you a chance to get to know your new coworkers in a more relaxed situation.

**6. Participate in group emails and chats.** There may be specific groups (email, Slack, etc.) for your team or group, so make sure that you are added and participate. These may be one of the main ways that information is communicated, so be sure to check them regularly.

**7. Personalize your work area.** If you have a desk or cubicle that is designated as yours (rather than just working in an open-space environment), take the time to add a bit of yourself to it. This might catch someone's eye, and they might then start up a conversation. Take time to notice if others have done the same to their own spaces, and feel free to compliment or ask questions.

**8. If you can move around, do it.** Conversely, if you don't have a designated work area, feel free to move around, so that you have the chance to interact with different people on a regular basis. Just be sure that you're letting others get their own work done, of course!

**9. Learn the etiquette of the break room.** Is there a certain way everything is supposed to be set up? Ask about it if there are no guidelines posted. Always make sure that you clean up after yourself (and wash anything that you've used) and leave things as you found them.

10. **Always be yourself.**  In the process of getting along with everyone and fitting in, remember that you don't have to change yourself in fundamental ways. You want to be able to continue being your own person. Others will appreciate you more if you're authentic, rather than trying to play a role to fit in, which will come across as false eventually.

> **"Far and away the best prize that life has to offer is the chance to work hard at work worth doing."**
>
> **—THEODORE ROOSEVELT**

# SEVEN TIPS FOR WORKING WITH YOUR NEW BOSS

**Working with a new boss can be rewarding, challenging, or anxiety-provoking, depending on how you approach the situation. You want to get started right with your new supervisor, so keep these things in mind as you ease into your new workplace.**

1. **Don't compare this boss with a previous one.** Each person is unique and brings their own style and process to a job. If you start comparing your new boss to someone else—for good or bad—you'll hinder the opportunity to establish a new working relationship. Be careful about prejudging the person and instead let things develop naturally.

2. **Show up on time and be ready.** Again, this seems obvious, but being punctual every day and ready to start work makes a good impression. Dress appropriately and be professional. Show your boss that you're committed.

3. **Take the time to get to know your new boss.** As with anyone, first impressions count, but allow some time to learn more about them. In your weekly meetings with your boss to check your own progress, this time will also give you a chance to get a better sense of who your boss is as a person and to understand their work style. On that note . . .

**4. Understand your boss's working style.** Some are very hands-on, while others leave their employees to work on their own and expect initiative and results from self-motivation. You'll probably be able to learn early on what your boss does (and they may even tell you), so be sure to work with that. If in doubt, ask a coworker or two.

**5. Take some initiative.** If you see a task or a problem, consider jumping in and getting to work on it, if it's appropriate to do so. Not waiting to be told what to do all the time is a great way to impress your new boss and shows you take your work seriously.

**6. Strive to do great work.** From day one, do your best and try to genuinely contribute. Your enthusiasm and commitment will reflect well on you and your boss *will* notice.

**7. Don't take things personally, at least at first.** If a problem comes up or you're criticized, try to not take it personally right away. It may have something to do with your boss's personality, or they may be having a bad day. But if it's something that happens repeatedly, then there's obviously a bigger problem. Either you're not understanding what needs to be done and how to do it, or this person has a problem with you. If this happens, you'll need to schedule a meeting with your boss and talk it out. Yes, that will be uncomfortable, but it's important to clear the air if any friction develops early on. You don't want this continuing!

# OFFICE POLITICS: WHAT TO EXPECT

Every place with human interaction will have a political element. This doesn't mean parties and ideologies. It means that some people will gravitate more toward others and factions may form, or ways of doing things may get set in stone, or rivalries may develop, or people have agendas and want to attain various things, or any number of other situations that in principle shouldn't have anything to do with your work, but probably will. This isn't necessarily a problem, but when you're stepping into a new environment, there will be countless interactions between people from the past of which you're not yet aware. How do you fit into this confusing tangle without being seen as taking sides? What if you have to take sides? And if you do form new friendships and alliances (which you definitely should), how can you be sure that they're the best ones to have (answer: you probably can't)? Here are some tips for navigating these potentially treacherous waters.

- **Watch, listen, and learn.** Your new workplace may be great, and everyone may get along just fine, or there may be some simmering tensions that you're not yet aware of. Keep an eye on things for a while and see how it develops, how people interact, and who speaks up against whom (if they do).

- **Be on your best behavior.** When you start a new job, make sure that you treat everyone with courtesy and respect. Don't give anyone a reason to dislike you or suspect you. You will undoubtedly make some friends faster than others, but conducting yourself properly toward everyone is essential (see the next section for more information). If you want to learn much more about office etiquette in general (always a good thing!), see *This Book Will Teach You Business Etiquette*, also in this series.

- **Keep things in perspective.** If you notice something—an altercation, a conflict, a snide comment—consider the source and the motivation behind it. Rarely is an office slight something that's worth getting too worked up about, unless you are being harassed or otherwise threatened, in which case by all means report it and take action. Quite a few of the more common causes of conflicts in an office—or among any group of people—are not worth getting too worried about.

- **Be careful about taking sides early on.** Until you know the whole story and can be clear about both sides and their positions, don't leap to the defense of one or the other too soon. You're new, and it's not a smart idea. Conversely, someone may approach you early on with gossip or other negative comments about someone else in the office or a group of people. This is very unprofessional, and with luck you won't have to deal with it. If it does happen, again, try to keep calm and keep some distance. Don't commit yourself to their version of events, and don't be so eager to fit in with a specific group that you allow yourself to be taken in with falsehoods.

- **Don't spread gossip.** Carrying on from the previous point, don't spread gossip or rumors that have been told to you. You'll have no real way of knowing if they're true or not, unless it's something that's happened to you, and even then, it's not a good idea to bring others into the midst of it. Keep cool and try to rise above it. If you do hear of someone being unfairly maligned, don't let it go further than you, and if you feel comfortable, consider reaching out someone, such as your boss, to try to put a stop to it.

- **What if someone says something about you?** This can be very hurtful, especially if you're new to the job. You want to fit in and have an enjoyable workplace. You'll have to decide what kind of message this gossip is spreading. It's possible that you can talk things out with the perpetrator (see "Eight Tips to Resolve Conflicts Successfully" on pages 117–18). But if it feels malicious, talk to your boss or the appropriate department; they may be able to put a stop to it. If it continues, you may want to consider filing a harassment complaint (see page 123). Of course, no one wants to do this at a new job, but it's something you'll need to keep in mind.

> # "Don't talk unless you can improve the silence."
>
> ### —*JORGE LUIS BORGES*

# SEVEN WAYS TO BE ON YOUR BEST BEHAVIOR AT WORK

It goes without saying that you need to conduct yourself professionally at work. You should give what you expect to receive and be respectful of those around you and of the job in general. Some people consider your first thirty days (or sixty, or even ninety) to be a kind of probationary period. And it's probably true that everyone will be watching you to some extent: your coworkers are trying to size you up, your boss is seeing how you fit in and if they made the right call in hiring you . . . but no pressure, right? Actually, there doesn't have to be much at all if you keep these things in mind.

1. **Have the right attitude and be ready to help out.** No matter what else is going on with you, you need to leave personal problems at the door and focus on your work. Your coworkers will appreciate it if you come to the job ready to contribute. Be friendly, be courteous, and be ready to do your job to the best of your ability.

2. **Introduce yourself at the right time.** If you are taking the initiative to meet new people, be careful about when and where you choose to do it. Cornering people in the restroom or as they're on their way out the door isn't a good look. Wait until they're in the break room,

or stop by their desk when they're not overwhelmed. Make the moment non-stressful, and you'll be remembered better. You don't want to seem pushy.

3. **Match your dress and attitude to the office.**
Going in wearing a suit when the rest of your coworkers are in jeans is just as bad a look as the other way around, and it signals that you're not interested in fitting in. It's fine to be an individual, but make the effort to meet them at the same level. This is also true for how you conduct yourself. If everyone is informal and calls the boss by their first name, it's good to go along with that. Take the "temperature" of the office mood and act accordingly.

4. **Don't get too personal too soon.** It's fine to talk a bit about yourself at lunch when socializing, but be careful about opening up too soon. If you're going through a rough spot in your personal life, seek out the friends and family you already have for help and support. New acquaintances are still getting used to you and probably don't want drama dumped on them at the start. After several months on the job, you might be OK with sharing a bit more, but be cautious at first.

5. **Be respectful of your new coworkers' time.** Don't bother them with unnecessary issues and problems, cling to them, or take up their time, unless there is a genuine need for their help. They'll probably give you your space to get on with your new tasks, so be sure to extend the same courtesy to them.

6. **Be respectful of your new coworkers in general.** Watch what you say in the first few weeks, especially. Don't interject too many opinions, don't bring up politics, don't tell off-color jokes (in some cases, this can be seen as sexual harassment), and for goodness' sake, don't talk about anyone behind their back. Your behavior will be noted and remembered.

7. **Don't mention your previous job, if you had one.** Unless it's directly relevant to the conversation or project, leave it out. No one cares, and if you keep mentioning it, it may make people wonder why you left in the first place. And most definitely don't bad-mouth that job, your old boss, etc.

[
**"I still get the jitters
every time I start a
new job! I love it—makes
you feel alive."**

**—CAMILLE GUATY**
]

# SEVEN TIPS FOR USING PHONES AT WORK

Phone calls are still a major feature of most work environments, even though we usually use our phones for just about anything but them these days! You may be assigned a specific phone and work number that you'll use for all phone communication. Etiquette for work phone use is essential and not hard to remember, so commit to these pieces of advice.

1. **Your work phone is for work only.** Whether it's a cell phone or a landline, don't make personal calls on it, unless you're specifically told that it's OK to do so.

2. **Don't talk too loud.** If you're at a desk or cubicle, be mindful that other people around you are also working and don't need to hear every detail of your conversation, even if it is work-related.

3. **If you have a speaker-phone option, don't use it.** Unless you can be in a private room for your conversation, this will just annoy your coworkers even more than you talking too loudly, because they'll have to listen to the other person, too!

4. **Make sure that your voice mail message is audible and clear.** If anyone phoning you is sent to voice mail, you want them to know they got the right person! Test out your message and have someone phone the number to make sure that it's all good.

5. **Don't use your personal cell phone at work, unless it's an emergency.** Save it for lunch, a break, or when you're off work. It's best just to turn it off at all other times. Don't leave it on vibrate; that will annoy not only you but also everyone around you.

6. **Don't bring your cell phone to the restroom to talk.** This is rude and in bad taste, especially if you're using your personal phone. Leave it at your desk.

7. **Don't bring your cell phone to meetings.** Even if you have a cell phone for work purposes, having it there runs the risks of calls and texts coming in and disrupting the meeting. Unless you're expecting an urgent, work-related call and inform the meeting organizer ahead of time, just leave it at your desk or have it turned off if it's with you. Sometimes, you may need to bring your phone in for a meeting-related purpose, and that is fine, of course.

> ## "Be sincere; be brief; be seated."
>
> **—FRANKLIN DELANO ROOSEVELT**

# YOUR FIRST OFFICE MEETINGS

> Meetings have a semilegendary reputation for being boring wastes of time. Unfortunately, the rumors are often true. As you ease into your new job, you'll undoubtedly have to attend them, maybe even from day one. Though they are inevitable (some studies suggest that they take up twelve hours or more of every week!), some are necessary, and it's fair to say that often you'll get out of them what you bring to them. Here are some tips for surviving your first meeting and the many more that will follow.

- **Show up ready and prepared.** You don't need to be a teacher's pet about this, but arrive on time or just a bit early, and be ready with whatever you've been asked to do, even if it's just taking notes. If you've been given an agenda or materials relevant to the meeting beforehand, make sure to bring them with you.

- **Introduce yourself.** Not everyone at the meeting might have met you yet. The meeting facilitator may make this a part of the opening of the meeting, offering you a welcome and inviting you to tell everyone a bit about yourself. By all means, do so, just keep it brief and make it relevant to the company.

- **Turn off your phone.** Yes, this again! Realistically, your phone should be off during working hours anyway, but even more so here. Having your phone buzz, beep, or ring during a meeting will look very bad at any time, even more so when you're new!

- **Pay attention to what others are saying.**
  Especially in your first few weeks, you can use these
  gatherings as opportunities to learn more. Your opinion
  and input may be requested, but always be prepared to
  take a bit of a back seat when you're new. Ask questions
  at the appropriate time, and make sure that everyone else
  has a chance to contribute.

- **Contribute when it seems right.** Unless it's an orientation,
  you're probably at the meeting because your input is valued. Feel free to
  contribute, just be mindful of when and where would be best. It may be
  that someone will ask you about your take on an issue, so don't hesitate,
  but be careful not to barge in or interrupt when others are talking.

- **What if you can't attend?** You will probably want to try to be
  present for everything in your first few weeks, but it's possible that on at
  least one occasion, you won't be able to attend a meeting because you are
  already busy with some other duty; they may be loading you up with new
  things to do in the first few weeks! This is fine, but let the meeting organizer
  know and ask if there is any important information you can pick up from
  them later. Offer to attend the next meeting.

# SETTING REALISTIC WORK GOALS FROM THE START

From your first week, you'll probably be assigned any number of tasks or set to work on projects. This is why you're here, and you want to dive into it, but also think about what your immediate and longer-term goals are. Here are some tips for keeping things grounded and realistic for yourself as you set about working to achieve your aims.

- **Define what your motivation is.** Is it just money? Are you trying to learn new skills? Do you want to move up the ladder at this specific company? Is this position a springboard to another job later? Are you eventually going to strike out on your own as a freelancer or entrepreneur? Whatever questions you have, they should be on your mind as you step into a new workplace. Define long- and short-term goals, and how they are both similar and different.

- **Clarify your role during the interview.** It's fine to ask what is expected of you during the first three months, the first six months, etc. You'll get a better sense of how working at this job will mesh with your own career goals. If the two converge, then it's a good fit.

- **If in doubt, ask!** The learning curve may be quite steep at your new job. You'll probably be required to absorb a lot in a relatively short amount of time, so never hesitate to reach out and ask those around you for help and advice. Ask your coworkers, ask your boss, ask any relevant departments. They're not going to resent you or be bothered. Be careful about overdoing it, though. If you can figure out some things on your own, give that a try first.

- **Be careful not to over-volunteer for tasks.** You want to be seen as enthusiastic and contributing to the team and the projects, but be careful about overextending yourself at the start. You don't want to be working on ten projects at once or staying at the office twelve hours a day to get work done. You were brought in for specific reasons, so stick to those reasons and do your best at those at the start. There may come a time when everyone will be required to pitch in more, stay late, or go the extra mile, and you'll be a part of that. By all means, take the initiative on a few things, but just be mindful of your workload and what you're able to do.

- **Ask yourself what skills you will need to learn.** You may receive on-the-job training for unfamiliar software or other company-specific items, but also investigate and see what else would be to your benefit to learn. What is needed only for this job, and what might be valuable for you in the future? The more knowledge you can accumulate, the better you will be setting yourself up for future success.

- **Be committed.** In order to achieve what you want, you'll have to make the effort to do it. If you want to have a good performance review, be promoted eventually, get a raise as soon as possible, or move up the hierarchy, all of these things will take time and planning. Write down your goals and make a commitment to working toward them. Add in as many details as you can about what you'll need to do to achieve them.

- **Be realistic.** There is only so much you can do in three months, or even a year. It's great to have ambitions, but make sure that they are realistic and can be achieved in the time frame you've set for yourself.

- **Track your progress.** Once you have a plan, stick to it and watch how you progress. Some things will take time, so try not to rush them. Be patient. Check off boxes or items on a list as you finish them. This will give you an idea of how you're doing, and also allow you to put tasks into chunks that are easier to complete. Don't forget to pat yourself on the back once in a while for a job well done!

- **Seek out feedback.** Get input from your boss and your coworkers. Are you meeting their expectations? What could you do to improve? Are you doing enough? Are you doing too much? Are there some areas that need more attention than others? Getting answers to these kinds of questions can help keep you on track as you keep your eyes on your goals.

[ CHAPTER 3: ]

# YOUR FIRST SOCIAL OUTINGS

When you start a new job, you'll meet a lot of new people. Depending on the size of your company, you'll see some of them a few times a year, if ever, while others will be in your sphere daily. It's not required (or even recommended) that these individuals become your new best friends, but you'll want to bond with your coworkers in meaningful ways. This will make your workplace flow much easier. As humans are social animals, it's inevitable that you'll be invited along for work outings and gatherings. This is a good thing! Take advantage of these to get to know your coworkers better and start building those connections from your first few days. It will make your transition into your new job that much easier.

# ACCEPT ALL LUNCH INVITATIONS!

It's very likely that you'll be invited out to lunch by your colleagues or your boss, maybe on your first day. This is an excellent chance to get to know people outside of the office, let your proverbial hair down a little bit, and be you, while they are presumably doing the same thing. Lunches can also be a great way to have a less-pressured business meeting or gathering to discuss a project. Here are a few things to keep in mind.

- **Accept lunch invites, even if you had other plans.** Did you bring your lunch on the first day? It's good to be prepared and not expect anything, but it's more important to take up that kind of invitation. Your lunch will probably keep in the refrigerator, and you can always eat it later. A first-day (or first few days') invite will give you an opportunity to get to know others better, and, just as importantly, a chance for them to get to know you. Sometimes, your new boss might even treat you to lunch in your early days. Never turn down a free lunch!

- **Be yourself.** At a casual lunch get-together, it's a perfect time to relax a little and show others who you are. Get talking about your hobbies, interests, background, etc., and encourage them  to do the same. As the new person, you may be in the spotlight and get more questions. This may be fine with you, or it may make you a bit uncomfortable. It's unlikely that anyone is doing this to put you on the spot; they just genuinely want to get to know you. Answer questions that you're comfortable answering and talk around the others, if you'd rather not share some details about yourself just yet.

- **Use the experience to get the lay of the land.** If a group of you is going somewhere for lunch, you can use it as a chance to get to know the neighborhood, if you're unfamiliar with it. Ask about the local shops and amenities, since you'll probably need to know about these later on.

- **Use lunches as a chance to network.**
  Though it's in the early days for your new job, lunch can be a good chance to think about making professional connections that may benefit you later on. This isn't purely self-centered; it gives you a chance to see who you might be able to reach out to and offer your own help and expertise as well. This is especially true if the lunch is attended by people who are not in your department or are not even at the same company.

- **Invite others out.** Once you've gotten to know
  the area a little bit, feel free to invite your coworkers out for lunch or coffee. Taking the initiative is a great way to show that you're a part of the team and want to be involved.

# HAPPY HOUR: WHAT TO DO

Going out for drinks is a long and almost hallowed tradition in the workplace. Gathering after a long day at work for beer, wine, or cocktails can seem like an important part of the bonding and socializing of a lot of jobs. Drinks and drinking culture are things that different people approach in their own ways. You may be totally happy going out to bars and restaurants and sharing drinks with coworkers at the end of the day or week, or it may not be your thing. Understand that either of these attitudes is acceptable. Here are some thoughts on the idea of happy hour and drinking as a social activity.

- **Learn when happy hour is, if there is one.** It may be that your coworkers have a designated day every week to go and grab drinks after work, or the process may be more informal, decided on the day, and it may only happen every few weeks, once a month, or something similar. If you're new to the job and get invited, do consider going along. It doesn't obligate you to go every time, but a chance to hang out with coworkers in a nonwork environment can be a great opportunity to bond and feel more like you're a part of the team. For future outings, it's fine to decline if you're tired or just don't want to go. And always remember that you can leave whenever you're ready. Making an appearance, even if only for a half hour, is more than enough social duty, if it's all you can cope with at that time.

- **What if you don't drink?** This is a legitimate concern. You may not drink alcohol for religious reasons, or you may be trying to avoid it (too much drinking in your past), or it may just be something you don't like. Any of these reasons is entirely valid, and you should never feel pressured to accept a drink that you don't want. Since you're the new person, be up-front and tell your coworkers that you don't drink alcohol. If you still would like to go along, you can drink sparkling water, soda, juice, or whatever you prefer to be a part of the get-together; your company should be the most important part, not what's in your glass. No one should object to this, and if they do, you may be dealing with a difficult coworker (see pages 117–18 for some ideas on conflict resolution).

- **What if you do drink?** This seems like a silly question, but think about it: you enjoy a good glass of alcohol and that's fine, but be very careful about how much you imbibe on one of these meetups. Know your limits and don't exceed them. Skip the shots, and have a beer or a glass of wine that you can sip over the course of the gathering. This is especially true if your boss or another supervisor-type is there, too. You don't want to say something you'll end up regretting later! Gossip travels at the speed of light, and if you make a spectacle of yourself, everyone will know about it soon enough.

- **Order food.** Even if it's just bar snacks, having some food in your belly will slow down the effects of the alcohol and give you a bit more tolerance.

- **Engage in the discussions and enjoy yourself, but watch out for certain topics.** Your coworkers may want to talk about anything but work, and that's actually a good thing. As a newbie, you need to be a bit careful about dipping your toe into the treacherous waters of office politics, at least for a while. If those kinds of discussions do come up, sit back, listen, and observe.

- **If someone offers to buy you a drink, it's OK to accept, but again, know your limits.** It's also a good idea to reciprocate.

- **Mind your words.** Always keep in mind that what you say and do is a reflection on you and the job, so especially in those first few weeks, watch what you say and do.

> **"Don't set compensation as a goal. Find work you like, and the compensation will follow."**
>
> **—HARDING LAWRENCE**

# OTHER OUT-OF-OFFICE CHANCES TO SOCIALIZE

You may receive invites to many social outings. These might be sponsored by the company or something initiated by your coworkers. Company events are pretty common, and they give employees a chance to have a bit of fun and be away from the pressures of the job for a little while.

- **Accept the invite if your company has a social event.** It may be anything from a Saturday picnic to a hike, to a day out rock climbing or kayaking. Unless you have a genuine objection or medical concern, it would be a good idea to accept the invitation, especially in your first few weeks and months. It will give you a chance to get to know everyone better, probably even your boss and superiors, and you'll feel more like you fit in. You'll probably won't be obligated to attend, but it will look good if you do. Actually, some workplace experts consider these kinds of events to be mandatory, even if you've been "invited," so keep that in mind.

- **Weigh your options if it's an employee get-together.** If the meetup is something more casual and voluntary, you'll have to decide whether it's something you want to do. You might be enthusiastic, or maybe you can't be bothered. If it's a department-wide event, then there may be some obligation or at least expectation, especially if your boss or supervisor is attending. If it's someone's birthday, it might be in your best interests to attend. You'd like for people to come to a birthday bash for you, wouldn't you? So even a token appearance will probably mean a lot to the other person.

- **What if you decide not to go?** So, the event is not mandatory, you've weighed the pros and cons, and you've decided that you're just too tired, too antisocial, you're washing your cat, or whatever. How can you gracefully bow out? Here are five tips.

1. **Thank them for the invite.** It's nice to be asked and thought of, so remember that. They weren't trying to impose on you; they wanted to include you. That's something to be grateful for.

2. **Be honest.** Tell them if you've already made other plans. And there's no need to tell them what those plans are, especially if they involve a bag of tortilla chips, salsa, and a streaming-service binge. Your time is your own. Just be sure that you don't make up excuses and then reuse them. People will catch on. If it's a spur-of-the-moment gathering, it's fine to just say you're too tired, because you may be. Some people have boundless energy, and if you don't, it's OK to embrace that.

3. **Let them know in enough time.** If it's an event that requires reservations, such as a dinner or a concert, it's rude to keep your host waiting to know if they need to book your seat or buy a ticket. Extend them the same courtesy you would want.

4. **Be willing to go along on another occasion.** You may not be able to cope with this particular outing, but it's going to look bad if you keep declining, even if these get-togethers are optional. So, you'll probably have to accept an occasional invite and tag along, even if it's not high on your list of priorities (that cat isn't going to wash herself, after all . . . actually, she will). Unless it's a time-oriented gathering (a movie, a concert), you'll probably be free to leave when you want. Often, making an appearance is the most important thing.

**5. Suggest alternatives from time to time.** Is there an activity you enjoy, or a place you like? Consider suggesting it as an option for a get-together in the future. That way, you're contributing to the group and showing that you're willing to be a part of it. And if they're into it, too, you'll get to do something you enjoy!

> **"By doing, you become employable. It doesn't matter what the job is; by working, you learn new things, meet new people and are exposed to new ideas."**
>
> **—KATE REARDON**

# BUSINESS-RELATED MEALS AND GATHERINGS: ELEVEN SURVIVAL TIPS!

It's possible that in your first month or two, you may get an invite to a business dinner or other get-together that's more formal than lunch, happy hour, or coffee. This kind of event may still be rather casual, or it may be a big deal. It may include senior members of the company and/or special guests from outside. Or it may be for your team or department exclusively. It may be casual or black-tie; there are so many possibilities! Here is some advice on how you should approach these potentially stressful and big-deal events without losing your cool.

1. **Ask how formal it will be.** Always find out what the dress requirements are. It's OK to overdress a little, which is certainly better than being underdressed.

2. **Be punctual.** In real terms, this means be a little early. Better to wait for ten minutes at the restaurant than face the embarrassment of showing up late and being shown to a table where everyone else is already seated. If you can't avoid being late (such as being stuck in traffic), always phone your host and let them know. If your host is late, give them at least ten to fifteen minutes before phoning to check in. They may be stuck in traffic, too!

### 3. Greet everyone with a friendly handshake.

You'll probably forget names if you're introduced to too many new people, but if you can try to use someone's name early on, you'll stand a better chance of remembering it.

### 4. Let your host and/or the most senior members of the party be seated first. In some cultures, this is mandatory. Follow protocol and take your seat when it is offered.

### 5. Sit up straight, keep your elbows off the table, and remember basic table etiquette. You know, all the things you were supposed to do as a child!

### 6. As with happy hour, approach alcohol with caution. Know your limits; it's OK to decline or to explain that you don't drink or are not drinking tonight.

### 7. Wait for senior members of the group to order food first. Also, take cues from others as to what kind of food you'll order. It's probable that your host is paying for the dinner, but don't just make that an excuse to order the most expensive item on the menu because you don't have to pay for it! Make sure to let the staff know about any special dietary requirements you might have. It's also fine to check up on this ahead of time.

### 8. Wait to eat until everyone has been served. Again, basic manners.

### 9. Leave your phone off. Unless you know that you might be needed in an emergency, don't take calls or answer texts during dinner! Seriously, they can wait. If a potential problem could happen, inform your host ahead of time in case you have to excuse yourself.

10. **Don't place things on the table.** Phones, handbags, even your napkin. Let the table be a place for food and drinks only. If you do have to excuse yourself, leave your napkin on your chair.

11. **Listen to the tone and flow of the dinner conversation, and take your cues from that.**  Things may start off very formally and transition into a more informal conversation, or they may be the opposite. Different cultures and even different companies may have differing approaches to this. The meal may have a specific purpose, or it may be a general get-together. Almost certainly there will be business topics to discuss, hence the term "business meal." But it's just as likely that conversations will drift into the social area as well. Be prepared and follow along with the direction that things take. Don't offer opinions on anything controversial, unless they are solicited from you. Also, be sure to spend more time listening and less time talking. As a new person, you're kind of there to be a sponge and soak up as much as you can. As always, watch how you behave, especially if senior members are sitting at the table. You don't want to make a bad impression in your first few weeks or months!

> **"Politeness and consideration for others is like investing pennies and getting dollars back."**
>
> **—THOMAS SOWELL**

# SIX TIPS ABOUT YOUR PERSONAL LIFE VERSUS YOUR PROFESSIONAL LIFE

When you start a new job, you will presumably have a core group of friends already, and your new coworkers will be just that: coworkers. Over time, you'll start to develop work bonds and even friendships with them, which is great! The question then becomes, how important are these colleagues to your outside life? It may be that you'll develop genuine, close friendships with one or more coworkers, but it's also important to recognize that having some distance between your work and personal lives can also be healthy. Work-life balance is a thing, and it's not necessarily a good idea to have them too mingled. Here are some suggestions for helping maintain that balance.

1. **Always be mindful of the fact that you're at your workplace to work.** Yes, that's stating the obvious, but it's important to remember. You likely will not be allowed to use your company email or phone for personal reasons (unless it is an emergency), and texting or checking your own phone is almost certainly prohibited until breaks or lunch. They're paying you, and they expect you to be present. So, excess socializing with work friends is off-limits, too.

2. **Watch your internet usage.**  Even more importantly than phone or email, surfing the internet for your own amusement while on company time is not likely to be tolerated. Unless you are doing something job-specific, leave it off until you get home. Instagram updates and cat photos will have to wait. Remember that some companies have IT departments that monitor your internet activity (search histories and such). Even if you've done nothing against company policy, it's still a violation of the reason why you're there. This is especially true in your early days at a new job.

3. **Keep an eye on your workload.**  If you're new, you may not have settled into a good balance yet, and some of your work may feel overwhelming. If you find that you're not finishing up everything you need to do by then end of the day, you should seek out your boss and mention it. It could be that you're getting a bit more than you can handle in the early stages, and the workload can be adjusted accordingly. You don't want to get into the habit early on of taking extra work home with you, unless that was a condition of your employment to begin with. Your company has a right to your time while you're at the office. But they don't own you outside of it. Be sure to set boundaries for this issue early on.

4. **Learn what the policy is concerning overtime.**  If you are asked to put in extra hours, especially as a new person on the job, make sure that you're being compensated fairly for it. In the run-up to a big project, a company may ask you to make some extra effort. But it's also perfectly fine for you to expect to be compensated for that. Your work contract or agreement may already have details about this situation, so be sure to review it.

## 5. Be careful about burning out quickly.

You may be young, enthusiastic, and excited to plunge into this new job, but be careful about making it your life, even if you are goal- and career-oriented. Young people get burned out in work situations all the time, and you need to be careful to pace yourself. As a newcomer, don't volunteer for everything or take on extra work just to make a good impression. Your own health and well-being are just as important.

## 6. Find the balance.
You won't be able to completely separate your work and personal lives, and you don't have to, but make sure that you take care of both aspects of your life, so that you can be happy in both. Imbalances and problems in one will affect the other.

[
# "Don't confuse having a career with having a life."

### —HILLARY CLINTON
]

# FRIENDS AND NEW COWORKERS: WHAT'S THE DIFFERENCE?

When you start a new job, you'll probably meet a lot of people, some of whom you'll be working with closely. Of course, you want to get along with them, even like them. You'll see them every day, you may regularly go out to lunch and other social occasions, and they will become an important part of your life. But are they really "friends"? Yes, however . . .

- **You are not obligated to form close friendships with work colleagues.** While you'll want to be on good terms with everyone, your personal life still belongs to you. Keeping some distance between work friends and "other life" friends has definite advantages. It lets you choose when and where you interact with coworkers outside of the office, and you won't feel so obligated to attend every social function. This is not to say that you shouldn't be social sometimes, but if it's the only thing you have going on, you might start feeling a bit trapped.

- **Research suggests that life/work boundaries are healthy.** If you are working with close friends, you may be more invested in their lives and their success than is good for you. Just as with office romances, being distracted by what a close friend in the office is going through can interfere with your own work duties and responsibilities. Of course, you can be concerned if someone in the workplace is struggling, but a bit of emotional distance might serve both of you better in the long run. At the very least, make sure that any discussions about problems happen off company time, but be mindful of your own need for space, too.

- **As with romances, close friendships can cause workplace problems.** What if you have an argument? What if one of you gets promoted and the other doesn't? What if your best friend is now your supervisor? Or the opposite? If one of you gets fired, will it reflect badly on the other person? What if the two of you are seen as a "block" by your coworkers, always siding with each other, of giving each other advantages? Will it lead to resentment? On that note . . .

- **A group of friends will tend to form an exclusionary bond.** Call it a clique, or whatever you like, if two or more of you are besties, it's going to be noticed. If you're always hanging out together and doing lunch but avoiding others, it might lead to resentment. Think about if you were not a part of that group and how it would feel if you then had to work with them on some important task. Would you feel welcome or like you were intruding?

- **Be casual friends instead.** Socialize, go to lunch, attend an occasional happy hour. Beyond that? Use your judgment. Is your coworker someone you'd want to go to a concert with? Go on a vacation with? Invite to your private birthday party? Maybe, but more than likely not. Only you can determine what distance is best, but be wary of focusing too much of your social life on your work environment.

- **This goes for social media, too.** It's probably fine to connect with each other on LinkedIn, but beyond that, be very careful about making connections and friends on Facebook, Twitter, Instagram, and other social media sites. Do you really want your coworkers seeing all aspects of your private life, your personal photos, and other information? Especially when you start a new job, this is probably a bad idea. At least take some time to get to know them better. If you receive an invite from a coworker to connect on a social media platform (beyond a business connection), consider carefully if you should accept it. It might not be the best idea.

- **You're not being aloof or rude; you're keeping a healthy distance.** Always remember why you're at your job, and make that your first priority. Over time, you'll develop some great relationships with people that may blossom into genuine friendships, but at the start, keeping up a few healthy barriers will be good for you.

> [ **"Motivation comes from working on things we care about. It also comes from working with people we care about."**
> —*SHERYL SANDBERG* ]

# ROMANCE AT WORK: NO. AND FURTHERMORE, NO

On your very first day, a certain someone flashed you a smile that made you go just a little weak. Or you shook someone's hand and it lingered for half a second too long. Or that cute person across the office just asked you out to lunch. Exciting? Sure. A good idea? No, not really. When you work with a group of people in close proximity, it's pretty much inevitable that certain feelings and attractions might get stirred up. And if you're single and looking, it might be very tempting to act on those feelings and attractions. But be careful, be very careful. Office romances are more often than not a bad idea, sorry to say. They may be great fodder for TV and movie comedies, but in real life, they can lead to disaster. Here are some reasons why you should avoid them, especially if you're new.

- **Your company may not allow it.** Given the legal quagmires of harassment and other complaints, your company may have decided that it's just not worth it, and they've instituted a ban on office romancing. This might seem harsh, but look at it from their point of view. Again, you're there to work for them, not find the love of your life, and the fallout of failed romances can lead to all kinds of unpleasant circumstances at work. If your company has this kind of policy, abide by it. If you break the rules and get caught, you may both face some kind of disciplinary action, up to and including getting fired. If you have an employee handbook, review it for any information, and if in doubt, ask!

- **Date a coworker and everyone will know.**
  This is unlikely to be something that you'll be able to
  keep secret. Gossip is uncontrollable, and you two will be
  the talk of the town, or at least the next happy hour that
  you're not invited to!

- **Dating a coworker can be a terrible distraction.** Seeing the
  person you're in love with every day at work might seem wonderful, but in
  the early throes of new passion, are you really going to be able to focus on
  your work? Will you be able to treat your beloved as any other coworker for
  purposes of working together? What if there's a conflict or disagreement,
  and the two of you somehow end up on opposite sides of a work issue?
  Can the two of you maintain a healthy distance and remain professional
  until after 5:00? Now, if the other person is in a different department, on a
  different floor, etc., this may not be as much of an issue, but you still need
  to be aware of what your company allows.

- **Dating a coworker could strain your office
  relationship.** What if you and your partner have a
  big fight over something? How is that going to translate
  into your office relationship? If the two of you end up in a
  strained situation, even if it's temporary, how likely is it
  that to cause problems at work and for your coworkers?
  Even worse, what if you break up and it's not amicable, but you still have to
  see each other every day? Just think about how awful that's going to feel. One
  or both of you may not want to show up at all. Is that fair to your colleagues?
  Your team? Would it make you want to quit just to not be around that person
  anymore? Is losing your great new job worth that hassle?

- **Dating your new boss:** No. Please don't ever do this. Just don't.

- **Watch your interactions in all cases.** Flirting can be fun, even if you have no intention of taking things any further, but be mindful of how your actions are perceived by others. You don't want to be giving someone the wrong impression, and if you're not careful, you may come across as creepy or harassing, which the last thing you want to do! Again, you may find yourself facing disciplinary action for something you never intended, which is most definitely not the way you want to start your new job!

- **Consider all the benefits of keeping romance outside of work.** With all of these examples, it should be obvious now why an office romance or fling isn't a good idea. Your personal life should be just that: personal. It gives you something important away from the job that you'll always have no matter what happens at work. When you have a bad day at the office, you'll have someone you can genuinely talk to about it in a safe and personal space, someone who isn't affected by company policies or worried about their own career there. And you can vent as much as you like. That alone makes keeping separate lives worth it!

# "I believe a balanced life is essential."

**—MARC BENIOFF**

# WHAT IF AN OFFICE PARTY IS COMING UP?

Office parties can be fun, or they can be stressful. They might be anything from a summer bash to a holiday extravaganza. These are the kinds of events where your attendance is usually mandatory, even if that's not explicitly stated. Forced fun may not seem like much fun, but it's something that you all have to do, and you'll feel better just going along and getting it over with. And sometimes they can genuinely be enjoyable! Here are some tips for making the most out of an office bash.

- **Assess what kind of party it is.** It may be a causal office shindig or a formal gathering at a hotel or restaurant (these are probably more likely during the holidays). Do you need to dress up? It probably doesn't hurt to make a little extra effort, unless you know it's a summer outdoor thing with live music and grilled food. Wearing formal wear to that would be a bit silly.

- **Ask if you need to bring food and drink.** In some cases refreshments are provided; in others, it's a potluck affair. Find out ahead of time.

- **Watch your alcohol intake.** Just like with happy hours, be wary of how much you are imbibing. Holiday punch tends to be an unholy concoction of multiple spirits and wines and other things all sloshed together in a big bowl, so be careful before indulging too heartily. At a summer bash, the beer may be free for the taking, but your dignity is also on the line. Don't do anything that would embarrass you. It's worth eating a generous amount of food if you can, so that any alcohol you drink takes longer to take effect. Find out if food is provided, or if it's only beverages. If it's just drinks, fill up on food before the party.

- **Watch what you say.** Yes, this is a party, but just like happy hours and other gatherings, you're still in the presence of coworkers and, in this case, you're kind of on company time. Bad-mouthing anyone or saying other negative things has no place here. Especially if you're new, keep it fun and social, and avoid office politics.

- **Don't drink or take recreational drugs (legal or otherwise) before the party.** Seriously, don't do it. For the same reasons you don't want to overdrink at happy hour, you don't want to make a scene. Your personal choices are your own, of course, but keep them to your personal life.

- **Don't go looking for a hookup.** These are especially notorious during the holidays. For all the reasons outlined above about office romances, a drunk or high fling could land you in a lot of trouble later on. Not only will people gossip, if it gets back to your superiors you could be in trouble. It's not the kind of statement you want to make in your first few months at the company! And if things are awkward between you and the other person afterward, it can create problems in the office, and even the potential for a harassment complaint, or worse, accusations of assault. Just don't do it.

[ CHAPTER 4: ]

# AFTER THE FIRST FEW WEEKS

The first few weeks may have been a bit stressful and
overwhelming, but you're settling in, getting used to the routine,
and making an impact. You have what it takes, and you're showing
others that, too. So, where do you go from here? What should you
be looking at as the next few weeks and months unfold?
This chapter looks at some of the best strategies and
attitudes to take with you going forward.

# SOLIDIFYING YOURSELF AS A PART OF THE TEAM

**If you were brought in for a specific task as part of a bigger project, you've already slotted into it and are working on your part. If you've joined a department, you've learned some of the ropes and are making your contribution. You know your coworkers, you've probably socialized with them a bit by now, and things are going well. Here are some suggestions for strengthening those bonds and making sure you stay integrated with the group.**

- **Continue to work with your mentor.** If you've found someone—or even more than one—who has been of help in getting you up to speed, continue working with that person. Their knowledge will continue to be helpful to you as you move forward. Again, think of them less as a teacher and more of a guide to the whole process.

- **Be willing to help out and do a bit extra.** Once you're more comfortable with how everything works, be willing to put in more of your time and effort if a project really needs to get done. You need to remain mindful of work-life balance, of course, but if some in your group want to get together after work to brainstorm ways to solve a problem, for example, be willing to go along, at least some of the time. Whether you put in actual overtime hours will be up to you and the terms of your work contract, but be up for going the extra distance at the start.

- **Build the relationships that count.** After a few weeks, you'll have a better sense of whom you work best with, whom you get along with, and who can most help you. Cultivate those relationships and work with them more often if you can. That's not to say that you should ignore everyone but those few people, of course! It's important to be cordial with everyone at the workplace for your own well-being. But people of like minds naturally gravitate toward each other, so keep your eye out for those people in your circle.

- **Take some initiative on socializing.** Once you've gotten to know people, ask one or more of them out for a working lunch. Maybe set up a weekly lunch or coffee meeting to assess how things are going, discuss future projects, etc. You can make it social and also useful to your job.

- **Always be thinking about the value you bring.** Remember why you were hired. What can you bring to this job? What can you bring to a particular problem? Don't be afraid to make suggestions, especially after you've gotten comfortable with everyone and the way the job works. Others are probably hoping for your input, if they don't outright ask for it.

- **Be careful about criticisms.** If your new job does things in a way that's different than what you're used to, it's just that: different, not necessarily worse. Try not to be too critical of the structure or the process. If you truly believe that you can simplify something or streamline it, then by all means, seek out your coworkers or your boss and make suggestions. Just be ready to listen to others and compromise. You may have a great idea, but someone else might be able to make it even greater.

# SETTING LONGER-TERM GOALS FOR THE COMING WEEKS AND MONTHS

**After your first week or two, you should already be thinking about what you want to achieve six months or even a year out. Take the time to write down some of your goals and hopes for the coming months and year. Use these pieces of advice as guides.**

- **Take stock of your professional situation.** Do you see this job as a place that you'd like to stay in for a while? Is there room for advancement and promotion in the manner that you would like? Or is this a job a stepping-stone along the way to something else? Being honest with yourself about this will help you get the most out of your time at your new job, whether you want to be there for a year or ten.

- **Understand your work responsibilities.** Obviously, you need to know what you're doing! If you're going to set new goals for yourself, be sure that you understand the full scope of your job so that you can plan accordingly. It's also entirely possible that new responsibilities will come your way as you settle into the job and your boss and coworkers get more comfortable working with you. View this as a chance to learn more and open new doors of possibility.

- **Always be networking.** It isn't enough to get to know your coworkers and boss. Try to reach out beyond your immediate group to other people in the company and even outside of it. Look for opportunities in lunches and coffee meetups to extend a friendly hand to people you don't yet know. You never know when you might meet someone  whom you can help or who can offer assistance to you at some point. This is especially true if you plan on staying at the same company or in the same industry for a while; the more people you know, the better.

- **Never stop listening or learning.** There will always be something new to learn and someone new to teach it to you. The more you can absorb, the better it will be for you in the long run. If a position at your company that you'd like someday requires certain qualifications, make the effort to learn or obtain them. You want to be priming yourself to be the best candidate for a raise, a promotion, or whatever else your goals may be.

- **Acquire new skills.** Related to learning, think of what skills would be best to help you get to the next level. Maybe you want to learn a specific programming language in the next three months to really get a handle on an ongoing work issue. Make this your goal and set up a reasonable schedule to achieve it. Would your ideal position require more formal education, such as an MBA? Investigate how it might be possible to do so part-time.

- **Track your progress.** It's always good to check in with yourself every month or more frequently to see how you're coming along. Maybe your goal was to bring in two new customers or clients for your company in your first month there. Did you achieve it? Could you have done even better? If not, why not? Always remember that when taking on bigger challenges and goals, it's best to break them down into smaller, bite-size pieces. Slow and steady really does win the race, so be patient with yourself.

- **Talk with your boss.** Setting work goals for yourself is great, but it's also a good idea to check in with your boss and see how realistic those goals are. If you want to bring in five new customers per month, for example, ask if this seems realistic; your boss is probably privy to more information and things you don't and can't  know yet. If you have a plan to help the company grow, is it doable in the time frame you're proposing? Can the company budget accommodate it? Before you commit yourself to goals that aren't going to be possible, make sure that what you want to do is achievable at this time.

> **"Don't be afraid to give your best to what seemingly are small jobs. Every time you conquer one it makes you that much stronger. If you do the little jobs well, the big ones will tend to take care of themselves."**
>
> **—WILLIAM PATTEN**

# CULTIVATING ONGOING WORKING RELATIONSHIPS

Your relationships with your new coworkers and boss will (we hope!) continue to grow and expand over time. After the initial period of getting to know each other and seeing how you fit in, there will still be ways that you can improve those relationships and your work environment in general. Also, be on the lookout for the opportunity to form additional working relationships with people in other departments or teams.

- **Think about what you can give, not just what you can get.** Working relationships are about much more than whatever advantage you can take from them. Always be thinking about how you can contribute and give back. Look for ways to help where you can, and check in to see how things are going.

- **Remember that your coworkers are human, too.** You know when you have a bad day? Everything is going wrong, your phone died, you have a headache, your partner broke up with you, you don't want to talk to anyone, or you just want to say, "Screw everything." Yeah, your coworkers have those days, too. Try to be understanding if someone seems to be in a bad mood or acting differently. If they are open to talking about it, then hear them out, but also respect their boundaries if they want their privacy. But above all, just remember that not everyone is going be 100 percent every day, including you.

- **Accept differences.** Not just differences in background, cultural norms, or political beliefs (and there will be those!). Someone may have a very different way of approaching a task or a problem than you do, and that's OK. Offer to share your own ideas, to collaborate, to try a combination of methods, but never assume that your way or opinion is the right one just because you've always done it that way or did it that way at a previous job. Be open to change and different points of view or methods.

- **Show your gratitude.** Always let your coworkers know that you appreciate them and their hard work. If you're new and they've accepted you into the group, be appreciative. Take one or more out for coffee from time to time, compliment their work, mention that you admire how they solved a problem. These little displays of gratitude and appreciation go a long way toward strengthening bonds, and you may well find that the good you give out will come back to you.

- **Forgive and forget, when it's appropriate.** At some point, you'll have a conflict with someone at work; it's probably inevitable. If you can work it out (see "Eight Tips to Resolve Conflicts Successfully" on pages 117–18), then do so. But once it's worked out, let it go and move on. Don't hold grudges. Being mature and taking the high road will be a much better approach in the long run. If the conflict is bigger or concerns issues such as sexual harassment or racial bias, however, by all means take appropriate action (see chapter 5). Being harassed or harmed at work is not something you ever need to forgive and forget about!

- **Reach out to others beyond your immediate circle.** You'll undoubtedly grow closer to your immediate coworkers as time goes on, but who else is there that would be good for you to know? Again, not just who would be good for you, but whom might you be able to help? Forming relationships across departments and different groups can be a great way to encourage future collaboration and participation. And that's only going to enhance your image and standing at the company.

# CHECKING IN WITH YOUR COWORKERS

You've worked with them for a month, or two, or three, so now would be a great time to check in with your new coworkers and see how things are going. This doesn't have to be a formal meeting; in fact, it might be better to do it over lunch or coffee, and it doesn't have to include your entire team all at once. One-on-one conversations can be great for exploring ideas and seeing how you're doing, how you're fitting in, etc. You may even get different answers from different people. If your answers are wildly different from person to person, you may have to sit and think about what that means. In any case, here are some questions and tips for getting coworker feedback.

- **How am I doing?** It seems obvious, but sometimes the direct question gets the most direct response. Ask how you've done so far and what you could do to be better. If they give you a vague answer, such as "you're doing fine," try to dig a bit deeper, but don't be pushy. Maybe you really are doing fine and that's all they feel they need to say.

- **What is the overall perception of me in the office/workplace?** Ask your colleagues to be honest. This question might be best asked in one-on-one conversations in private, where you'll be more likely to get an honest answer. This might be a bit nerve-racking because you're putting yourself out there for less than flattering replies, but if you feel that things are going well so far, you probably don't have too much to worry about, and you won't hear anything that will shock you. On the other hand, if you've been sensing some tension, this would be a good chance to clear it up.

- **What do you think I could do to improve?** If you ask different people at different times, you may get different answers. This could be very interesting, and some answers may even contradict others. It will give you a better sense of how your coworkers see you. Since they have different responsibilities than you, maybe they see you as focusing on one aspect of the job more than another and feel you need to balance your attention between tasks a bit more.

- **Am I fitting in well?** Check in to see how you're settling in with the team or the department. Maybe your work is fine, but they'd like you to be a little more social with the group. Make the commitment to do an extra lunch once in a while or attend an extra after-work function from time to time.

- **Take everything they say on board and give it consideration.** If you've solicited your coworkers' honest opinions, you'd better be prepared to take them! It's unlikely that anyone is saying anything to be mean (and if they are, you have another problem; see "Eight Tips to Resolve Conflicts Successfully" on pages 117–18), so be open to suggestions if things aren't going as well as you thought they were. In most cases, this probably won't be a big deal and will only help you improve.

# CHECKING IN WITH YOUR BOSS

You may be working at a company that has periodic performance reviews, say every six or twelve months. These are normal and nothing to be alarmed about. Still, if you've been having weekly check-ins with your boss, you might want to ask for a mini-review of your own after a few months, to make sure that you're on track and doing the right things. The idea is to ask your boss what's working and what could be improved. Taking this kind of initiative is a great way to show your commitment to the job and keep the lines of communication open. Here are some questions to ask your boss and actions to take at this kind of meeting.

- **How am I doing so far?** Again, it seems simple and obvious, but be straightforward. You want an honest answer and evaluation. Again, make sure that your boss goes into more detail than just "fine, great!" You want the good and the less good, so that you can get an honest assessment of your performance so far.

- **What can I do to improve?** Showing that you are aware of room for improvement is a great exercise in humility, and indicates that you're willing to learn and grow with the company. No matter how great you're doing, there will almost always be some room for improvement somewhere (sorry, but it's true!). Ask for specifics and make a plan with your boss to track your progress.

- **What would you do in [whatever your situation is]?** If
  you are working on a task or project and are feeling a bit stuck, this can be
  a great chance to engage your boss in getting their advice for how to tackle
  it. This is especially true if they have past experience in the same area.
  Having your boss advise or mentor you from time to time can be a great
  way to connect and show your commitment to improving.

- **Is there anything else that would be useful
  for me?** Is there additional training that could benefit
  you? Is there an upcoming conference or round table
  that would be good for you to attend? Are there any
  professional organizations or networks you should join?
  Ask about any other opportunities that could be useful
  for you, with the idea that the more you know, the more
  you'll be able to contribute.

- **Focus on any results you've gotten so far.**
  If you've scored some early wins, now is the time to bring
  them up again. Being diligent about day-to-day activities
  is something that you're expected to do, so don't go in
  wanting praise for that. Instead focus on results and show
  how your routine tasks led to something better. Did your
  phone calls bring in three potential new clients? Awesome!
  Did poking around in the computer system reveal a problem
that no one else has noticed? Great! Your boss will be impressed if you're
doing the job well, and the results will speak for themselves.

# CHECKING IN WITH YOURSELF

Now that you've been here for a little while, sit with yourself and ask how things are going. Take some time to evaluate everything so far, what's been good, what's been not so good, and what could be improved. Here are some questions to keep in mind.

- **How am I doing at my job?** Assess your performance and be honest with yourself. Are you living up to your own expectations? What have you found the most challenging? What has been easy? Is anything better or worse than you expected?

- **How am I doing in my own life?** Ask yourself about your work-life balance. In the first few weeks or months, you may have been giving your new job much more attention than anything else, but at some point you'll start to notice that things are out of balance if you overdo it. Are you getting enough sleep? Are you feeling overly stressed? Are you neglecting your friends and family? What can be done to smooth things out?

- **Is the job what I expected it to be?** We go into new positions with a lot of hopes and expectations, and some of these will be met, while others may not be. Ask yourself about what has turned out as you thought it would, and what has been different. The job might be different in a good way. Have you been pleasantly surprised by anything? Are there any difficulties that you didn't anticipate? If so, how are you dealing with them?

- **What can I do to make sure things work out?** You've talked with your boss and with your coworkers and gotten their feedback, but are there any other things you can think of that you need to do or do better? Is there anything that you're overdoing that you could scale back on? What beyond their suggestions can you do to meet expectations but also ensure that you're not taking on too much all at once? What strategies do you have for the next three months, or six months, and beyond?

> **"There are two kinds of people, those who do the work and those who take the credit. Try to be in the first group; there is less competition there."**
>
> **—INDIRA GANDHI**

# WHEN THE NOVELTY WEARS OFF AND THE HONEYMOON'S OVER

The first month or two (or even six) has gone by at your new job, and things are going great: you're succeeding, even exceeding, and then . . . something happens. Maybe it sets in gradually, maybe it hits you all at once, but you start to feel less excited and enthused. Maybe things are starting to be a little bit more of a slog and you're waiting for the workday to end, or maybe your morning commute is getting more tiresome (this can especially be true if it's getting into the colder months of the year). For whatever reasons, the grace period is wearing off, and the reality that this is a job for the long term starts to set in. This situation is pretty normal; novelty always gives way to routine. What can you do to keep your interest up and bring the same levels of enthusiasm to your job that you had a few months ago? Here are some ideas.

- **Be aware of the pressures you are under, including those you put on yourself.** You want to impress early on—you want to show your value and prove that they were right to hire you. But be careful about taking on too much work or working too long at the end of the day. Being enthusiastic and wanting to contribute is not the same as running yourself into the ground. If you're being overloaded with too much work, talk to your boss about ways to make it more manageable. And if you're overloading yourself, stop doing it!

- **Assess your expectations.**  It's inevitable that the novelty will wear off, but when it does, go back and think about why you took this job, and what you're still hoping to get from it. If you came here from a previous job that you didn't like, research suggests that when you hit this stage, the letdown will be even more intense, because you were hoping to get away from one or more dissatisfying things in your old job. Remember that every situation brings advantages and disadvantages, and even if you love your new job, some things about it will probably annoy you eventually.

- **It might be about you.**  This is not to blame you, but research has suggested that even employees who are well-adjusted, have made friends with their coworkers, and are meeting their expectations can go through a period like this. A lot of it has to do with the expectations you bring to the job, and this is normal. The good news is that this mini-burnout seems to affect most employees and is not necessarily a sign of a bigger problem.

- **Practice self-care.**  This may seem clichéd, but make sure that you are getting enough sleep and enough to eat. If you're grabbing snacks while working late, and then skipping breakfast to get in early, it's going to take a toll on you, no matter how healthy you feel you are. If you're up until 1:00 a.m. every night and the alarm goes off at 6:30, you're going to feel it later in the day. Eating well and sleeping are vital to good health, and no job is worth sacrificing that for.

- **Make sure to take breaks.**  This is another form of self-care, but if you're glued to a computer for much of the day, be sure to stand up and wander around for a short time every ninety minutes or so. Just the act of a bit of movement and stretching can help you feel a bit revitalized. Go out for lunch and take a walk somewhere. If you engage in exercise in your personal life, don't neglect it.

- **Prioritize if you're feeling overwhelmed.** If there are too many emails in your inbox, or too many texts or chat messages in want of your time, give your attention to the ones that are most urgent. It might be that some of them can wait a while.

- **Remember what attracted you to this job to begin with.** It's likely you went for this job because there were many things about it that appealed to you. The good news is that those things are still there. Remind yourself of the good aspects of the job and why you wanted it. Look for ways to rekindle that feeling in your day-to-day operations.

> **"Take care of yourself: When you don't sleep, eat crap, don't exercise, and are living off adrenaline for too long, your performance suffers."**
>
> **—EV WILLIAMS**

# HOW TO BE A SUCCESSFUL EMPLOYEE

> Being good at your job doesn't mean just showing up on time and following orders. Success also isn't just about salary or job title. Your goal should be to make yourself useful, even indispensable, to the company by bringing your best to the proverbial table. Success is also defined by your own well-being. Working yourself to death for an ungrateful company in order to try to win a promotion or raise is not a good example of success.

- **Maintain a good attitude.** So much of what we encounter in life can affect us based on how we react to it. At the risk of sounding like a self-help lecture, it's important to go in with a good, healthy attitude about your job, surroundings, coworkers, boss, and more. If anything is negatively affecting any of these, it's going to affect how you view your job and whether or not you even want to do it. Always try to prevent problems, if you can. Resolve conflicts peacefully (see pages 117–18), and keep yourself in a good frame of mind.

- **Show your company and your boss that they made the right decision in hiring you.** Be ready and willing to dive in and accept new challenges, keep your promises, deliver things on time, and generally be excellent at everything you do. Sounds simple, right? Well, it does take effort (that's why you're there, after all!), but if you're following the advice in this book, you'll have many useful ideas to help you succeed. Do your best by being your best.

- **Get involved in the company in other ways.** Many large companies have several activities beyond the work itself: they sponsor charity events, they have sports teams, they host celebrations and parties, etc. Take the opportunity to volunteer once in a while to be on the planning committee for one of these activities or ask how you can help in other ways. If you're at a larger company, it can be a great chance to meet people you might not otherwise come into contact with, and your enthusiasm and commitment will likely be noticed by higher-ups at some point.

- **Keep track of your successes.** Along with tracking your progress, this is a great way to remind yourself of what you've achieved so far. It creates a sense of accomplishment and satisfaction, and reminds you that it's not all just work. Reward yourself with a deluxe coffee or a slice of cake. Pat yourself on the back for a job well done, and use your successes as a spur to do more and better in the future. After all, more successes equals more cake, which is always a good thing!

- **Continue to maintain a good work-life balance.** Again, this is essential. The only way that you'll be able to continue doing a good job and not quickly fall into burnout is to know when your job ends and your life begins. It's essential to keep a good balance between the two. Working fourteen-hour days and sleeping very little might seem cool at the beginning, but it's going to get old very quickly—and your health and mental state will start to suffer. Make time for your own interests and activities, your friends, your family, and those things that are just as important to you. Eat well, sleep well, and take care of yourself in all ways. If you want this job to last, you need to be able to bring your best to it in the long run!

- **Always keep your perspective and sense of humor.** Most things can be pretty funny, if you think about them long enough. And much of what seems to be hugely important probably needs to be taken down a peg or two. This is **not** to say that you should slack off at your job or not take it seriously; far from it! But try to keep everything in perspective and remember the things in life that are really important: your family, your friends, your health, your well-being. Everything else comes and goes. If you keep that in mind, then you can take your job seriously and give it your all, and make yourself into an employee that your boss, colleagues, and you will be proud of!

[
**"You will never feel fully satisfied by work until you are satisfied by life."**

—*HEATHER SCHUCK*
]

# CHAPTER 5

# WHAT IF THERE ARE PROBLEMS EARLY ON?

Starting a new job can be exciting, thrilling, overwhelming in a good way, and of course you want it to be a good experience. In most cases, it probably will be. But sometimes things can go wrong, even early on. The job may not turn out to be all it was cracked up to be, or maybe you were even deceived about what your role would be. And the unfortunate truth is that you may encounter difficulties with others that are more than just small annoyances or things you can ignore. Issues like sexual harassment and racial bias are still a problem in workplaces, despite the gains that have been made in recent decades. But know that the law is on your side if you are facing these difficulties, and you have every right to feel safe and secure in your new job. If you do come up against any problems, this chapter offers some advice on how to deal with them.

# SIX ACTIONS TO TAKE WHEN FEELING LIKE YOU DON'T FIT IN

A few weeks or a month or two may have gone by, and you've settled in well enough. Except . . . something or several somethings seem off. Maybe you're just not clicking with your coworkers, maybe you're finding them difficult to get along with, or maybe there's a bigger problem. Here are some ideas for taking stock of your situation and solving the problem. If there are larger problems to address, see pages 130–31 for what to do when the job isn't what you hoped it would be. Otherwise, here are some suggestions.

1. **Assess what you think the problem really is.** Are you not getting along with your new coworkers? Does your new boss rub you the wrong way? Is the culture of the office different from what you're used to? Are you much older or younger than most of your coworkers? Do you come from a different racial, ethnic, or religious background than most of the people in your workplace? Any of these things and much more can leave you feeling isolated and out of place.

2. **Determine if the problem is external or internal.** This can be a bit difficult and require some soul-searching, but ask yourself if the issue is with others or you. It may be that you are simply more introverted or not as much of a people person as some others are. If you're a bit uncomfortable meeting new people or simply work better on your own, that's OK. But knowing this will help you to see the situation better. If

someone is genuinely bothering you, please refer to pages 117–18 for how to resolve workplace conflicts.

3. **Ask yourself if there is an economic issue.** Maybe your new coworkers like going out and spending money on lunch every day, or they go to happy hours and order expensive drinks. You, on the other hand, are trying to save money right now, what with it being a new job and all. If you keep turning down invitations, it may give you the reputation of being antisocial, when in fact you just want to be frugal. It's okay to bring this up with coworkers; just tell them you're trying to save money in your first few months and maybe offer some suggestions for less expensive outings.

4. **Take note of what's working, not just what isn't.** Remind yourself of the things that are going well, and use those as a place to start from when trying to fix other issues. If the work itself is going smoothly, it's just a social issue; then you at least have that. Maybe you get along with some people better than others. This is totally normal, so try to focus on those relationships at the start.

5. **Reach out more.** Again, this can be difficult for some people, and if it's not your cup of tea, that's OK, but if you are so inclined, try making the effort to ask coworkers out to lunch or coffee. If there's a break room, try socializing there a bit more. Join conversations if you feel comfortable. The goal here is not necessarily to form lifelong friendships, but to make the workplace cordial and accepting. If you are seen as being open and friendly, others will notice and respond in kind.

**6. Imitate.** This suggestion is more controversial, but it might be worth your time to observe and then work to act more like your coworkers. If the workplace is very competitive, you might have to make yourself more like that. It may just be a matter of seeing how your coworkers interact and trying to be a bit more like them. If the office is more casual and people joke around, but you come from a more traditional workplace, this may take a bit of getting used to, and vice versa. But never feel that you have to change who you are to fit in! If there is a real disconnect, altering your personality isn't going to fix that.

> **"The highest reward for a person's toil is not what they get for it, but what they become by it."**
>
> **—JOHN RUSKIN**

# SIX TIPS WHEN YOU HAVE PROBLEMS WITH SOMEONE YOU WORK WITH

You hope and want to get along with your coworkers. Not everyone is going to become a great friend, and, as mentioned, that's as it should be. Your coworkers are a different part of your social circle than your personal friends. Still, you want to be able to get along with everyone, be cordial, and have a sense that you can at least work with them. Unfortunately, there may be times when there's someone in your workplace that you just don't like or they just don't like you. It's not necessarily anything that either of you has done (or maybe it is?), but if you don't fix it, and soon, it could grow into something worse and more problematic. Here are some ways to keep that from happening.

1. **Be careful not to get angry (or at least don't show it).** Keeping your temper in check will help in the long run. If you lose it and blow up at someone, it's just going to make you look like the problem.

2. **Try to speak to the person directly, if that's not too uncomfortable.** Neither of you know each other that well yet, and there may be any number of reasons why you're butting heads. One or both of you may have personal problems that are unconsciously bleeding

over into the workplace. Having a civilized chat may be just enough to dispel the issue. If you're willing to look at the situation from their point of view, they may do the same for you. You may find that they're more reasonable than you had first thought.

3. **Remain civil and respectful.** You must do this even if they don't. Again, don't do anything that will cast you in a bad light, especially since you're the new kid on the block. You don't want to get a reputation as being a troublemaker, even if the other person started it, and to be honest, your new coworkers are probably going to be more likely to believe the other person than you, unless they are a known troublemaker. On that note . . .

4. **Try to see how others in the workplace react to this person.** Without being too obvious, maybe try to observe how this person works with others. It may be that they are obnoxious toward everyone, in which case, it's not personal, even though it's still a problem. Or maybe you're being singled out as the new person in some sort of childish behavior. But if this person gets along with everyone else, you'll have to dig deeper to see what the problem is.

5. **Watch what you say.** You may be tempted to say something about the problem to your new coworkers, if you're getting along with them. This may or may not be a good idea, depending on how well you trust them, but remember, you're new, so you have to navigate office politics carefully. Also, rumors and gossip spread like wildfire in office environments, so if you are having problems with someone, word of it will travel fast. You don't want coworkers picking sides, especially against you.

**6. Speak to your boss, if you can't resolve it.** If you've tried working it out with the difficult person and aren't getting anywhere, it may be time to go and see your boss, who's going to want to know how you're doing anyway. It's in their best interest to ensure that a new employee is fitting in well, and if it's having a bad effect on your work, your boss needs to know. Be careful how you present it, though; you don't want to be seen as a troublemaker or the new person whining about things. And don't just assume that because you're new, the boss will side with you. They will probably sit you both down and try to work things out.

[
**"If we manage conflict constructively, we harness its energy for creativity and development."**
*—KENNETH KAYE*
]

# PROBLEMS WITH YOUR BOSS

What happens if the difficult person at your work turns out to be your boss? They may have been great when you were hired, great for the first week, but then things started going wrong. This may feel like a worst-case scenario, and, with luck, you'll never have to face it, but it does happen, and you'll have to approach it with care if you want to stay at your new job.

- **Figure out what the problem is.** This is crucial. It may be a work issue: the person micromanaging or not helping you enough. They are giving you too much work all at once, or they're not that good at their job. Or it may be personal: they are blunt or moody, or they are rude or indifferent. The nature of the problem will definitely determine what you have to do to fix it.

- **Try to see if anyone else has the same problem.** Again, as the newbie, this might be a bit tricky. You don't want to just go off attacking your boss to people who may have worked with them for years. You're better off watching your boss's behavior toward your coworkers. If it seems relatively good, the problem might be personal, but maybe they're that way toward everyone.

- **Try to understand why your boss may be acting this way.** As with the difficult coworker, you can't possibly know what's going on in their personal life, but consider that they may be having family problems, or the business may be in a rough spot, or maybe they've been given a new set of responsibilities. You won't likely be able to learn about any of this, but keep it in mind. Also remember that your boss is only human, and maybe they're not happy with their own situation at the moment.

- **Record any incidents that concern you, both involving you and your coworkers.** Be specific and include dates and times, if you can. If your boss has done this kind of thing before, the company may have other complaints on file, and yours will be helpful to add to those.

- **Ask to speak to your boss directly, if this seems like a solution.** As with a difficult coworker, there may be any number of reasons why you are butting heads that have nothing to do with you. If your boss is amenable to talking things out, then certainly consider taking that option.

- **Do what you can to keep it from affecting your work.** This may be very difficult, but if you can continue with your work as usual, then try to do so. Don't give your boss any further reasons to make things hard on you. Minimize your contact, if possible, and don't let it consume you, unless it gets really bad.

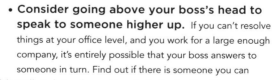

- **Consider going above your boss's head to speak to someone higher up.** If you can't resolve things at your office level, and you work for a large enough company, it's entirely possible that your boss answers to someone in turn. Find out if there is someone you can contact confidentially to bring the problem to their attention. You may not be the only one who's complained. And by all means, if you are facing sexual harassment or any kind of discrimination, do not hesitate to report your boss to the appropriate authority.

- **Ask for a transfer.** Again if you work in a company that is large enough, you may be able to request a transfer to another department, if they can accommodate you. Bear in mind that this may not be possible during your first few months, or there may be other reasons why you can't move right away. Since you are a new hire, they may be less willing to accommodate you than if you've been there for a while.

- **Consider leaving, if all else fails.** Obviously, this is not a great option, but you may feel you have no choice. It's heartbreaking to start a new job only to feel you need to leave a few weeks or a few months later. But if the situation is not resolvable, you may be left with no choice.

> **"When conflict becomes a win-lose contest in our minds, we immediately try to win."**
>
> **—THOMAS CRUM**

# EIGHT TIPS TO RESOLVE CONFLICTS SUCCESSFULLY

**If you have a difficult coworker or boss, you may be able to talk things out, as we've seen in the previous two sections. But how do you do that? Here are some tips for making a difficult situation a bit easier.**

1. **Don't put it off.** It may feel icky, it may make you squirm, but the longer you leave things, the worse the situation is likely to become. Take the time you need to prepare (assembling facts, practicing what you want to say—write it down!), but when the time comes, face up to it.

2. **Go in with the idea that this is something you can resolve to the satisfaction of both parties.** Don't try to score points or get a "win." You want both sides to be happy with the outcome.

3. **Agree to actually meet in person at a specific time.** No chat, no emails, no conference calls. Sit down together in a room across the table and speak to each other. This may seem terrifying (and it probably will to the other person as well), but it's the only way to be sure that things get ironed out.

4. **Listen to the other person.** It seems simple, but by giving the other party time to say what's on their mind, you are showing respect and that you're willing to meet them halfway. Just be sure that they return the favor and give you

equal courtesy. If they don't, then you can be fairly sure that you're not the problem and you're just dealing with a difficult person.

5. **Consider using a mediator.** Some companies will provide these, or you may want to bring in someone from the outside that you are both comfortable with. Professional mediators can keep things focused and help you work toward a solution.

6. **Figure out what the problems are and see if you also agree on other points.** Agreements can help you resolve the issue better. Speak up about what's bothering you and why, and let the other person do the same. You may discover that you've done something, even unintentionally, that has caused a problem. If so, own up to it, apologize, and commit to fixing it. Just be sure that the other person is giving you the same level of respect.

7. **Work out a plan together to fix the problem.** You may need to meet again or simply resolve to change how things are done so that the issue doesn't become an issue in the future. You'll probably want to check in and monitor your progress along the way to a solution. Just make sure that you stick to the plan, and make sure that they do as well.

8. **Be prepared if the problem doesn't get solved.** It may be that even after talking and working through things, the issue remains. This can be for any number of reasons. Mediation from a higher-up may be called for, or someone in your company may offer (or impose) a solution.

# WHAT TO DO ABOUT A COWORKER'S INAPPROPRIATE BEHAVIOR

Questionable behaviors are one of life's most unpleasant situations, even more so if they're happening in your workplace. The next two sections will focus on sexual harassment and racist actions, but there are other behaviors that might be a problem for you. If you encounter anything early on in your new job, you need to be prepared.

- **Try to lead by example.** If you are always on your best behavior, people will notice. So, if difficulties come up, be sure to react to them in appropriate and professional ways. Simply treat others as you would like to be treated.

- **Never accept behavior that involves bullying or intimidation.** You do not have to put up with this—not from coworkers or your boss. Collect information if you need to, and be prepared to report it to the appropriate department or government agency if it continues or gets worse.

- **Try to avoid gossip.** It may seem harmless and even fun, and it's almost certainly inevitable, but it can do real harm. If it happens a lot, it might even be worth bringing it up to those engaging in the gossip and reminding them that it can be hurtful. Of course, if you're the new person, you may have to tread lightly here. If the gossip concerns you for any reason, you have the right and even a duty to make it stop, using the methods of conflict resolution outlined above.

- **Never make derogatory and disparaging comments about anyone.** This should be a no-brainer, but sometimes when people get on the gossip train, bad things happen. Topics such as someone's appearance, religion, gender, sexual preference, and personal life are out of bounds. They are no one's business, so don't engage in any talk that brings them up. And if someone is saying things like this about you, you may want to consider reporting it.

- **Keep your work phone and email for work only.** Again, this seems obvious, but if someone uses the office email to send a vulgar joke, an inappropriate image, or other questionable material, it can be construed as harassment. Don't forward these emails, don't send them yourself, and if it happens to you, consider following the guidelines for conflict resolution to make sure the sender knows why it was wrong and doesn't do it again. If it keeps happening, report it.

If you experience harassment of any kind, you have legal recourses. See the Resources section of this book for more information.

# IF YOU EXPERIENCE SEXUAL HARASSMENT

Sexual harassment has come to the forefront of the news cycle in recent years as more brave victims are stepping up to recount instances of abuse, some dating back decades. This kind of behavior afflicts all levels of society, but fortunately you do have recourse. Sexual harassment in the workplace is illegal. The law is on your side, but here is some additional information for dealing with this upsetting and hurtful experience.

- **Remember that your employer is obligated to keep all employees safe.** Further, your company must take steps to prevent harassment and to ensure that it doesn't happen again. This is nonnegotiable.

- **Know what your own level of tolerance is.** Different people may have different definitions of what they find acceptable. This doesn't excuse any inappropriate behaviors, of course, but it's important to know what you believe. Never let anyone tell you that you're being "too sensitive" or "it was just a joke," if you don't feel that's the case.

- **No one has the right to call you names.** "Babe," "honey," "sweetie," and so on are very often considered condescending, and you are not obliged to put up with them. Pet names in this context are unprofessional and potentially offensive.

- **You do not have to accept any unwanted physical contact or invasion of your space.**
Even if the person meant nothing by it (or claims so after the fact), your personal space is yours alone. Touching you, cornering you, making innuendos, telling off-color jokes, anything that makes you uncomfortable is off-limits.

- **You have a right to feel what you do.** If someone's behavior was inappropriate to you, you never need to feel guilty about feeling bad about it. It is not your fault, and you didn't do anything to "lead someone on," no matter what they might say. You are always entitled to feel safe and respected in your office or workplace, and you are entitled to your own bodily autonomy at all times—no exceptions.

Usually, there are two recognized types of sexual harassment—quid pro quo and hostile work environment. Here is what each entails:

- **Quid pro quo** is when you are offered the chance to exchange sexual favors for advancement. This can include benefits like hiring, raises, and promotions, but also negatives, such as the threat of being fired, a demotion, some kind of blackmail, and so on.

- **Hostile work environment** refers to anything of a sexual nature that makes you uncomfortable. This includes physical advances, unwanted touching, someone being in your personal space in an unwanted way, jokes of a sexual nature (in person or via email), images sent by email (such as pornography), any comments about the attractiveness of you and other employees, etc.

- **Men and women harass both men and women.**
Sex and gender may play a role, but there may also be some kind of power dynamic going on (boss to employee, senior worker to new worker). The harassment may even come from a client or customer. No matter what the source, it is not acceptable.

- **It's normal to feel angry, scared, embarrassed, humiliated, and confused, and it's not your fault.** You are entitled to feel what you do, and don't let anyone tell you otherwise.

- **You have the right and the freedom to respond in the way that seems best to you.** You may seek out legal advice or report the incident to higher-ups, or you may not. If you are afraid of retaliation (such as losing your job or being demoted), this is a legitimate concern. Whether or not you decide to report the incident, remember that you do have resources and support available to you. See the Resources section for more information.

- **Please don't hesitate to tell your friends, family, a therapist, or even legal counsel if you are suffering and need to talk.** You are not alone.

> **"Standing behind predators makes prey of us all."**
> —*DASHANNE STOKES*

# IF YOU EXPERIENCE RACISM OR OTHER BIASES

Racism and other forms of bigotry are unfortunately still far too prevalent in modern society. If you are a part of a minority group (racial, LGBT, or other protected category), you already know that discrimination can take many forms. This is a difficult subject and cannot be summarized adequately here, but the following points will give you some information on what to watch for and how to protect your rights.

- **Discrimination in any form is illegal,** but that doesn't keep it from happening. And it may not be blatant or obvious. Remarks, jokes, or snide comments from coworkers or your boss all contribute to an atmosphere of discomfort. More serious examples might include being passed over for a raise or a promotion, or being fired or demoted unjustly, but bias can also come in other forms. Comments about your language or appearance, for example, may not be intended to be hurtful, but they can make you feel uncomfortable, or singled out. None of this is acceptable.

- **If you experience any instances of discrimination** or see it happening to a coworker, take note of it and write down the details: time, date, place, nature of the incident, and who was involved. Keep this evidence on file, away from your workplace. If the situation escalates, you may be called on to provide that evidence, and the more you have, the better your case will be.

- **If it seems appropriate, report the incident to your boss,** supervisor, or another department, if there is one in place to handle complaints. Do this in writing and keep copies for yourself. Most companies will have strict rules against this behavior and will investigate the complaint seriously; not doing so could put them in all kinds of legal trouble. If your boss is a part of the problem,  then by all means go over their head. Just because you are new doesn't mean that you have to put up with being mistreated.

- **Racial discrimination in the workplace is illegal.** Each province has its own laws regarding enforcement of antibias laws, so you will need to investigate to see what they are in your particular province. Your company is required to investigate all complaints. If they fail to do so, they are breaking the law.

- **If you are concerned about backlash or retaliation, know that you are not alone.** It may make the decision to come forward more difficult, but what is happening to you is illegal, and any additional actions taken against your reporting an incident are also illegal. If you are struggling with what to do, reach out to friends and family for advice, and consider taking legal counsel.

This short guide won't be able to answer all of your questions and concerns about this very troubling topic. If you need more information, see the online references in the Resources section of this book for much more information. And be sure to reach out to others in your social circle for support.

# WHAT IF YOU HAVE A MEDICAL OR FAMILY EMERGENCY?

Most of the time, we don't think about bad things happening, but unfortunately accidents and other unforeseen things happen and can throw us off. If you or a loved one faces a medical or other emergency that requires you to leave work and/or be away from it, here's what to do.

- **If something happens, be sure to tell your boss as soon as possible—and, if you need to, any appropriate coworkers.** If you have to leave work, explain what has happened and, if you have any idea, how long you might need to be away. Your boss will probably be understanding; if you experience any difficulties with this, remember that your family comes first, not devotion to some misplaced work ethic. You can smooth things out at work later, and any retaliation or punishment is illegal.

- **If you are injured or hit with any kind of health problem that prevents you from coming into work, notify your boss as soon as possible.** Make sure that a friend or family member has your work information and can relay a message, if necessary. One of them will also need to be your emergency contact, if you are injured on the job.

- **Canada has a variety of sick leave laws (rather than one countrywide set), which vary widely from province to province.** You will need to check on your province's particular laws to see what applies to you. The amount of sick or emergency leave time can vary from a few days to as much as half a year.

- **Time off is often unpaid.** Policies vary from company to company. However, you may be able to qualify for benefits under the Canada Pension Plan or Employment Insurance.

- **Qualification for leave varies from province to province.** Factors that determine your eligibility include the size of the company you work for, how long you have worked there (there may be a minimum time to qualify), and the nature of the illness or injury.

- **Personal versus care leave times are often different.** Generally, you will qualify for more time off if you are leaving to take care of a sick family member. Again, circumstances will dictate the exact amount of time.

- **Disabilities are protected.** If your leave is caused by a disability, you have protection under human rights legislation. If your employment is terminated during this time, you may be able to claim discrimination. The same may hold true if you take time off work to care for a family member with a disability.

- **Your employer is not allowed to deny you leave.** They also cannot retaliate, fire, or demote you, or engage in any other practice that would prevent your return.

Medical emergencies and other crises are some the most stressful things that we will ever have to deal with. No matter how healthy we are, bad things can happen. Prepare by expecting the best, but always be informed and ready in case something happens.

# WHAT ARE YOUR LEGAL RIGHTS?

**If you face harassment of any kind on the job, see something illegal happening, see someone else facing discrimination, or have problems getting your company to take the matter seriously, there are a number of resources to help. The following list of agencies and legal information will get you started, and see the Resources section for website addresses.**

The Canadian Human Rights Commission exists to educate and inform about rights and what to do if you experience sexual harassment, racist behavior, and various other forms of discrimination, including being based on age, disability, religious beliefs, national origin, sexual orientation, First Nations status, and other categories. The website also gives information on how to complain if you experience discrimination or harassment, whether at the federal level (for federal employees) or to your specific province. If someone at your company engages in these practices, or the company ignores your complaints or concerns, or you experience retaliation or wrongful termination, this is the organization to contact.

The Labour Program maintains standards for federal worker and employer rights.

Different provinces have their own employment laws, and the majority of Canadian workers will fall under these laws. All employers must place an Employment Standards Act poster in a visible location at your workplace. These laws will vary somewhat in terms of things like minimum wage, overtime, and so on, but all must adhere to basic standards of antidiscriminatory practices and employee rights. Check with your individual province's laws and see what applies to you.

You have the right to join, form, and participate in unions. It is illegal for your boss to fire you (or threaten to fire you) for joining or forming a union, and they cannot favor employees who don't support unionizing, shut down your place of employment, or offer to bribe you if you agree not to join.

> **"Be open to the amazing changes which are occurring in the field that interests you."**
> **—LEIGH STEINBERG**

# WHAT IF THE NEW JOB IS NOT WHAT YOU THOUGHT IT WOULD BE? SIX SUGGESTIONS

So, you're a few weeks into the new job and things . . . aren't great. You're finding that this is not what you expected, there's more responsibility than you anticipated, or you're worried that you don't have the knowledge or skills to do the job successfully. This is a worst-case scenario, but it does happen sometimes. So what can you do?

1. **First of all, don't panic.** Things may seem overwhelming or hopeless, but there's a decent chance that if you were good enough to get the job, then you're good enough to do it, unless you totally misrepresented yourself at your interview (don't do that!). Remember that you're new to the situation, and there's going to be  a learning curve (names, procedures, the layout, etc.), even if you're very qualified (and of course you are!). You may have entered at a chaotic time: Is a big project underway? Are you one of several new hires? Take in the whole situation first and see if there's a bigger picture.

2. **Allow yourself a bit of time to adjust.** Following from remaining calm, give yourself a little more time to adjust. If you're feeling overwhelmed in your first three days, that's probably normal. If you're still feeling that way after four weeks, there may be a bigger problem. Try to settle in for a while and see what happens.

3. **Speak to your boss.** Schedule a time to sit
down with your boss and discuss your concerns.
There may have been some miscommunication at the
start, and they may not know that you're struggling.
Be specific about what you need to say and write it down beforehand.
State your concerns, and be prepared to listen and take in suggestions for
improvement. If you are experiencing discrimination or abuse of any kind,
then refer to the earlier sections of this chapter to take appropriate action.

4. **Commit to working with your boss to solve the
problem.** It's worth giving it a try. You've gotten this far, so don't throw
in the towel just yet. There may have been some misunderstandings about
your role and responsibilities. Be willing to work with your boss to solve
the problem. Commit to, say, another month before making your final
decision.

5. **Be prepared to leave, if necessary.** This is a last resort, and
one that you almost certainly don't want to face, but it may come to that
if you can't find a better solution. You may experience many negative
feelings about this: guilt, anger, frustration, disillusionment. Just know that
your own well-being is more important than any workplace. There will be
other jobs, and one that will be a better fit, but there is only one you, and
you have to take care of yourself!

6. **You may have an exit interview.** Some
larger companies have an HR department that will
want to interview you when you leave. If this is the
case, give them specific reasons for why you are
leaving, and be polite and professional at all times.
Your feedback may actually help them not make the
same mistake going forward, so that they can hire a
better fit for the job.

# RESOURCES

While every attempt has been made to give a quality and timely introduction to the kinds of information you should know as a new employee, if you would like to go deeper into the subject (and there is definitely more to learn about than what's discussed here!), the following books and websites will be very helpful in filling in the picture. From successfully navigating your first few weeks to thinking about longer-term plans, there is plenty more to learn, so dig in and make yourself as prepared as you can; happy reading!

# FURTHER READING

There are many books available with information to help ease you into a new job. Many are more management-oriented, but here is a selection of titles that are general in nature and will give you additional guidance for your first ninety days and beyond.

Advanta Publishing, *90 Day Motivational Journal for Starting a New Job: Inspirational Guided Self Help Journal, Log and Notebook for Women to Explore, Strive and Thrive* (Advanta Publishing, 2019).

Roy Blitzer, *Find the Bathrooms First!* (Crisp Publications, 1999).

Marshall Goldsmith, *What Got You Here Won't Get You There: How Successful People Become Even More Successful* (Hyperion, 2007).

Dawn Graham, *Switchers: How Smart Professionals Change Careers and Seize Success* (Amacom, 2018).

Robert Hargrove, *Your First 100 Days in a New Executive Job: Powerful First Steps on the Path to Greatness* (Independently published, 2011).

Alexandra Levit, *New Job, New You: A Guide to Reinventing Yourself in a Bright New Career* (Ballantine Books, 2009).

Heather McCollum, *Work Like a Pro: Your Guide to Finding, Accepting, and Starting a New Job* (Independently published, 2018).

Robert Moment, *Starting a New Job: Career Planning and Job Promotion Tactics for Motivated New Employees* (Moment Group, 2019).

Jen Sincero, *You Are a Badass®: How to Stop Doubting Your Greatness and Start Living an Awesome Life* (Running Press, 2013).

Milo Sindell, *Sink or Swim!: New Job. New Boss. 12 Weeks to Get It Right* (Adams Media, 2006).

Sharon Vargas, *New Job Survival Guide: How to Start Your New Job Successfully, Stress Free and with Confidence in Today's Complex Work Environment* (Independently published, 2017).

Michael D. Watkins, *The First 90 Days: Proven Strategies for Getting Up to Speed Faster and Smarter* (Harvard Business Review Press, 2013).

Michael D. Watkins, *Master Your Next Move, with a New Introduction: The Essential Companion to* The First 90 Days (Harvard Business Review Press, 2019).

# ONLINE RESOURCES FOR HELP WITH LEGAL ISSUES AND QUESTIONS

The following is a list of websites that give more detail on such topics as employee rights, harassment issues, and other legal problems. These are mainly government sites and have extensive amounts of information. These sites will be very helpful if you need further information and assistance dealing with work-related problems. Laws about discrimination and labor rights will vary from province to province, but will not be substantially different than the federal laws listed in some of these links.

## Canadian Government: Employment and Social Development Canada

From the website: "Employment and Social Development Canada (ESDC) works to improve the standard of living and quality of life for all Canadians. We do this by promoting a labour force that is highly skilled. We also promote an efficient and inclusive labour market."
**canada.ca/en/employment-social-development.html**

## Canadian Government: Employment Insurance benefits and leave

Information on a variety of benefits that you may be eligible for.
**canada.ca/en/services/benefits/ei.html**

## Canadian Government: The Labour Program

From the website: "The Labour Program is responsible for protecting the rights and well-being of both workers and employers in federally regulated workplaces. We work closely with provincial and territorial governments, unions, employers, international partners, and other stakeholders to promote fair, safe and productive workplaces and collaborative workplace relations."
**canada.ca/en/employment-social-development/corporate/portfolio /labour.html**

# Canadian Government: Rights in the Workplace

A resource that includes information and links on the following topics: The Canadian Human Rights Act, The Employment Equity Act, The Canada Labour Code, rights for foreign workers, and The Human Rights Maturity Model.
**canada.ca/en/canadian-heritage/services/rights-workplace.html**

# Canadian Government: Sick leave, work-related illness and injury leave, and long-term disability plans

This page offers extensive information on what to do if you need to take time off due to an illness or injury, with a comprehensive FAQ.
**canada.ca/en/employment-social-development/services/labour-standards /reports/sick-leave.html**

# Canadian HRC Equal Employment

From the website: "The Canadian Human Rights Commission conducts audits to determine if employers are meeting their legal obligations to offer equal employment opportunities to four designated groups: women, Indigenous persons, persons with disabilities and members of visible minorities."
**chrc-ccdp.gc.ca/eng/content/equal-employment-opportunities-0**

# Canadian Human Rights Commission

Those who feel that they have been discriminated against can file a complaint or receive information from this site on how to take their complaint to the appropriate authority.
**chrc-ccdp.gc.ca/eng**

# Public Service Alliance of Canada

The PSAC website offers information on unions and employee rights regarding joining and participating in unions.
**psac-ncr.com/union-rights/our-rights-under-law**

For more online help with any of the topics covered in this book, a search of the subject you want to read more about should return a good number of results, some of which will go into more detail than a book this size can allow. Many are US-based sites, but the information is generally applicable in Canada, too, unless it deals with specific labor laws and practices.

# ABOUT THE AUTHOR

**Tim Rayborn** is a writer, educator, historian, musician, and researcher, with more than twenty years of professional experience. He is a prolific author, with a number of books and articles to his name, and more on the way. He has written on topics from the academic to the amusing to the appalling, including medieval and modern history, the arts (music, theater, and dance), food and wine, business, social studies, and works for business and government publications. He's also been a ghostwriter for various clients.

Based in the San Francisco Bay Area, Tim lived in England for seven years, studying for an M.A. and Ph.D. at the University of Leeds. He has a strong academic background but enjoys writing for general audiences.

He is also an acclaimed classical and world musician, having appeared on more than forty recordings, and he has toured and performed in the United States, Canada, Europe, North Africa, and Australia over the last twenty-five years. During that time, he has learned much about the business of arts and entertainment, and how to survive and thrive when traveling and working in intense environments.

For more, visit timrayborn.com.

INDEX

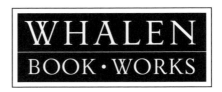

## PUBLISHING PRACTICAL & CREATIVE NONFICTION

Whalen Book Works is a small, independent book publishing company based in Kennebunkport, Maine, that combines top-notch design, unique formats, and fresh content to create truly innovative gift books.

Our unconventional approach to bookmaking is a close-knit, creative, and collaborative process among authors, artists, designers, editors, and booksellers. We publish a small, carefully curated list each season, and we take the time to make each book exactly what it needs to be.

We believe in giving back. That's why we plant one tree for every ten books sold. Your purchase supports a tree in the Rocky Mountain National Park.

*Get in touch!*

Visit us at **WHALENBOOKS.COM**
or write to us at
68 North Street, Kennebunkport, ME 04046

# TAKE YOUR CAREER
# TO THE NEXT LEVEL!